# OBJECTIVE
## KET

Annette Capel
Wendy Sharp

Student's Book

D0716827

CAMBRIDGE UNIVERSITY PRESS
Cambridge, New York, Melbourne, Madrid, Cape Town, Singapore, São Paulo, Delhi

Cambridge University Press
The Edinburgh Building, Cambridge CB2 8RU, UK

www.cambridge.org
Information on this title: www.cambridge.org/9780521541497

© Cambridge University Press 2005

This publication is in copyright. Subject to statutory exception
and to the provisions of relevant collective licensing agreements,
no reproduction of any part may take place without the written
permission of Cambridge University Press.

First published 2005
10th printing 2009

Printed in Dubai by Oriental Press

*A catalogue record for this publication is available from the British Library*

ISBN 978-0-521-54149-7 Student's Book
ISBN 978-0-521-54150-3 Teacher's Book
ISBN 978-0-521-54151-0 cassette set
ISBN 978-0-521-54152-7 CD set (audio)

Cambridge University Press has no responsibility for the persistence or
accuracy of URLs for external or third-party Internet websites referred to in
this publication, and does not guarantee that any content on such websites is,
or will remain, accurate or appropriate. Information regarding prices, travel
timetables and other factual information given in this work are correct at
the time of first printing but Cambridge University Press does not guarantee
the accuracy of such information thereafter.

Cover design by Dale Tomlinson

Designed and produced by Kamae Design, Oxford

# Map of Objective KET Student's Book

| TOPIC | EXAM SKILLS | GRAMMAR | VOCABULARY | PRONUNCIATION (P) AND SPELLING (S) |
|---|---|---|---|---|
| Unit 1 Friends 8–11<br>1.1 Friends for ever<br>1.2 Borrow this! | Paper 2 Listening: Part 1 | Present simple: *be, have*<br>Questions in the present tense | Adjectives describing feelings<br>Personal possessions | (P) The alphabet |
| Exam folder 1 12–13 | Paper 2 Listening: Part 1 | | | |
| Unit 2 Shopping 14–17<br>2.1 For sale<br>2.2 Shopping from home | Paper 1: Part 1 (Reading)<br>Paper 2 Listening: Part 3 | *How much ...?*<br>*How many ...?*<br>*some* and *any* | Shopping and shops | (P) /ɑː/ *car*, /eɪ/ *whale*, /æ/ *apple*<br>(S) Plurals |
| Exam folder 2 18–19 | Paper 1 Reading and Writing: Part 1 (Reading) | | | |
| Unit 3 Food and drink 20–23<br>3.1 Breakfast, lunch and dinner<br>3.2 Food at festivals | Paper 1: Part 6 (Writing)<br>Paper 2 Listening: Part 5<br>Paper 1: Part 4 (Reading)<br>Paper 1: Part 9 (Writing) | Present simple<br>Adverbs of frequency<br>Telling the time | Food and drink<br>Celebrations<br>Dates (day and month) | (S) Contractions<br>(P) /ɪ/ *chicken*, /iː/ *cheese* |
| Writing folder 1 24–25 | Paper 1 Reading and Writing: Part 6 (Writing) | | | |
| Unit 4 The past 26–29<br>4.1 A long journey<br>4.2 A trip to remember | Paper 1: Part 4 (Reading)<br>Paper 2 Listening: Part 5 | Past simple<br>Past simple: short answers<br>Past simple + *ago* | Nationalities | (S) Regular verbs in the past simple<br>(P) Regular past simple endings |
| Units 1–4 Revision 30–31 | | | | |
| Unit 5 Animals 32–35<br>5.1 A trip to the zoo<br>5.2 An amazing animal | Paper 2 Listening: Part 3<br>Paper 1: Part 5 (Reading) | Lists with *and*<br>Conjunctions *and, but, or, because* | Animals<br>Collocations with *do, make, take* and *spend* | (P) List intonation<br>(S) *their, there, they're* |
| Exam folder 3 36–37 | Paper 1 Reading and Writing: Parts 2 and 5 (Reading) | | | |
| Unit 6 Leisure and hobbies 38–41<br>6.1 Theme park fun<br>6.2 Free time | Paper 3 Speaking: Part 2<br>Paper 2 Listening: Part 4<br>Paper 1: Part 3 (Reading)<br>Paper 1: Part 9 (Writing) | Comparative and superlative adjectives<br>Comparative adverbs | Leisure activities<br>Descriptive adjectives and adverbs<br>Telephoning | (S) Comparative and superlative adjectives<br>(P) /ə/ *camera* |
| Exam folder 4 42–43 | Paper 2 Listening: Parts 4 and 5 | | | |
| Unit 7 Clothes 44–47<br>7.1 The latest fashion<br>7.2 Your clothes | Paper 1: Part 4 (Reading)<br>Listening for information<br>Paper 1: Part 3 (Reading) | Simple and continuous tenses | Clothes<br>Adjectives to describe clothes | (S) *-ing* form<br>(P) The last letters of the alphabet: w, x, y, z |
| Writing folder 2 48–49 | Paper 1 Reading and Writing: Part 7 (Writing) | | | |
| Unit 8 Entertainment 50–53<br>8.1 A great movie<br>8.2 Cool sounds | Paper 1: Part 5 (Reading)<br>Paper 2 Listening: Part 1 | Modal verbs 1: *must, had to, may, can, could* | Films, music | (P) Short questions<br>(S) Mistakes with vowels |
| Units 5–8 Revision 54–55 | | | | |

| TOPIC | EXAM SKILLS | GRAMMAR | VOCABULARY | PRONUNCIATION (P) AND SPELLING (S) |
|---|---|---|---|---|
| Unit 9 Travel 56–59<br>9.1 Making holiday plans<br>9.2 Looking into the future | Listening for information<br>Paper 1: Part 3 (Reading)<br>Paper 1: Part 7 (Writing) | The future with *going to* and *will* | Travel, space | (P) /h/<br>(S) Words ending in *-y* |
| Exam folder 5 60–61 | Paper 3 Speaking: Parts 1 and 2 | | | |
| Unit 10 Places and buildings 62–65<br>10.1 Inside the home<br>10.2 Famous buildings | Paper 2 Listening: Part 2<br>Paper 1: Part 2 (Reading) | The passive – present and past simple | Furniture, materials<br>Opposites<br>Buildings | (S) Words ending in *-f* and *-fe*<br>(P) Dates (years) |
| Exam folder 6 66–67 | Paper 1 Reading and Writing: Part 4 (Reading: Right, Wrong, Doesn't say) | | | |
| Unit 11 Sport 68–71<br>11.1 Living for sport<br>11.2 Keeping fit | Paper 1: Parts 3 and 4<br>Paper 2 Listening: Part 5<br>Paper 1: Part 6 (Writing) | Word order in questions<br>Verbs in the *-ing* form | Sport and sports equipment<br>Fitness | (P) /b/ *basketball*, /v/ *volleyball*<br>(S) *gu-*, *qu-* |
| Writing folder 3 72–73 | Paper 1 Reading and Writing: Part 9 (Writing) | | | |
| Unit 12 The family 74–77<br>12.1 Family trees<br>12.2 Large and small | Paper 2 Listening: Part 3<br>Paper 1: Part 4 (Reading: Right, Wrong, Doesn't say) | Possessive adjectives and pronouns<br>Subject, object and reflexive pronouns<br>*Everything, something, anything*, etc. | People in a family | (P) /aʊ/ *cow*, /ɔː/ *draw*<br>(S) Words ending in *-le* |
| Units 9–12 Revision 78–79 | | | | |
| Unit 13 The weather 80–83<br>13.1 Sun, rain or snow?<br>13.2 Too much weather! | Paper 2 Listening: Part 2<br>Paper 1: Part 5 (Reading) | *(Not) as ... as*<br>*Enough* and *too* | Weather | (P) Unstressed words with /ə/<br>(S) *to, too* and *two* |
| Exam folder 7 84–85 | Paper 2 Listening: Part 2 | | | |
| Unit 14 Books and studying 86–89<br>14.1 Something good to read<br>14.2 Learn something new! | Paper 2 Listening: Part 4<br>Paper 1: Part 3 (Reading) | Position of adjectives<br>*Rather than* | School subjects, education | (P) Silent consonants<br>(S) Words that are often confused |
| Exam folder 8 90–91 | Paper 1 Reading and Writing: Part 3 (Reading) | | | |
| Unit 15 The world of work 92–95<br>15.1 Working hours<br>15.2 Part-time jobs | Paper 1: Part 4 (Reading: multiple choice)<br>Paper 2 Listening: Part 3 | Present perfect<br>*Just* and *yet* | Work, jobs | (S) Words ending in *-er* and *-or*<br>(P) /ð/ *clothes*, /θ/ *thirsty* |
| Writing folder 4 96–97 | Paper 1 Reading and Writing: Part 8 (Writing) | | | |
| Unit 16 Transport 98–101<br>16.1 Journeys<br>16.2 A day out | Paper 3 Speaking: Part 2<br>Paper 2 Listening: Part 1 | Modal verbs 2: *must, mustn't, don't have to, should, need to, needn't* | Transport<br>Collocations with transport<br>Directions | (P) Weak and strong forms<br>(S) *i* or *e*? |
| Units 13–16 Revision 102–103 | | | | |

# Content of the KET examination

The KET examination consists of three papers – Paper 1 Reading and Writing, Paper 2 Listening and Paper 3 Speaking.

There are four grades: Pass with Merit (about 85% of the total marks); Pass (about 70% of the total marks); Narrow Fail (about 5% below the pass mark); Fail. For a Pass with Merit and Pass, the results slip shows the papers in which you did particularly well; for a Narrow Fail and Fail, the results slip shows the papers in which you were weak.

## Paper 1 Reading and Writing 1 hour 10 minutes
(50% of the total marks)

There are nine parts in this paper and they are always in the same order. Parts 1–5 test a range of reading skills and Parts 6–9 test basic writing skills. You write all your answers on the answer sheet.

| Part | Task Type | Number of Questions | Task Format | Objective Exam folder |
|---|---|---|---|---|
| Reading Part 1 | Matching | 5 | You match five sentences to eight notices. | EF 2 |
| Reading Part 2 | Multiple choice (A, B or C) | 5 | You choose the right words to complete five sentences. | EF 3 |
| Reading Part 3 | Multiple choice (A, B or C) AND | 5 | You choose the right answer to complete short conversational exchanges. | EF 8 |
| | Matching | 5 | You choose five answers from eight to complete a conversation. | |
| Reading Part 4 | Right / Wrong / Doesn't say OR | 7 | You answer seven questions on a text that is up to 230 words long. | EF 6 |
| | Multiple choice (A, B or C) | | | EF 10 |
| Reading Part 5 | Multiple choice (A, B or C) | 8 | You choose the right words to complete eight spaces in a short text. | EF 3 |
| Writing Part 6 | Word completion | 5 | You decide which words go with five definitions and spell them correctly. | WF 1 |
| Writing Part 7 | Open cloze | 10 | You fill ten spaces in a text such as a postcard with single words, spelled correctly. | WF 2 |
| Writing Part 8 | Information transfer | 5 | You complete a set of notes or a form with information from one or two texts. | WF 4 |
| Writing Part 9 | Short message (5 marks) | 1 | You write a short message, such as a note or postcard (25–35 words), which includes three pieces of information. | WF 3, WF 5 |

## Paper 2 Listening   about 30 minutes, including 8 minutes to transfer answers

(25% of the total marks)

There are five parts in this paper and they are always in the same order. You hear each recording twice. You write your answers on the answer sheet at the end of the test.

| Part | Task Type | Number of Questions | Task Format | Objective Exam folder |
|------|-----------|---------------------|-------------|-----------------------|
| Listening Part 1 | Multiple choice (A, B or C) | 5 | You answer five questions by choosing the correct picture, word or number. There are two speakers in each short conversation. | EF 1 |
| Listening Part 2 | Matching | 5 | You match five questions with eight possible answers. There are two speakers. | EF 7 |
| Listening Part 3 | Multiple choice (A, B or C) | 5 | You answer five questions about a conversation between two speakers. | EF 9 |
| Listening Part 4 | Gap fill | 5 | You complete five spaces in a set of notes. There are two speakers. | EF 4 |
| Listening Part 5 | Gap fill | 5 | You complete five spaces in a set of notes. There is one speaker. | EF 4 |

## Paper 3 Speaking   8–10 minutes for a pair of students

(25% of the total marks)

There are two parts to the test and they are always in the same order. There are two candidates and two examiners. Only one of the examiners asks the questions.

| Part | Task Type | Time | Task Format | Objective Exam folder |
|------|-----------|------|-------------|-----------------------|
| Speaking Part 1 | The examiner asks both candidates some questions. | 5–6 minutes | You must give information about yourself. | EF 5 |
| Speaking Part 2 | The candidates talk together to find out information. | 3–4 minutes | You are given some material to help you ask and answer questions. | EF 5 |

## 1.1 Friends for ever

1 Here are some reasons why friends are important. Look at them together. Which is the best reason? Write three more reasons together.

**Twelve reasons why friends are great!**

1. Friends are always there for you.

2. It isn't fun to watch television alone.

3. You get funny text messages from them.

4. They don't tell you lies.

5. You have someone to go shopping with.

6. Friends don't forget your birthday.

7. It's great to go on the PlayStation together.

8. You can chat about football for hours.

9. Your best friend has your favourite ice cream in the fridge.

10. They help you with your homework.

11. Parties without your friends aren't good!

12. Friends make you laugh.

## GRAMMAR EXTRA

*be* and *have*

2 Copy and complete the verb boxes. Some words are in exercise 1.

| The verb *be* | The verb *have* |
|---|---|
| I *am, I'm, I'm not* | I *have, I've, I haven't* |
| You .................... | You .................... |
| He, She, It .................... | He, She, It .................... |
| We .................... | We .................... |
| They .................... | They .................... |

## Pronunciation

3 🎧 Listen and write down the letters you hear. What famous names do the letters spell?

1 _ _ _   _ _ _ _ _ _ (a popular film)
2 _ _ _ _ _ _ _ _   _ _ _ _ (a film star)
3 _ _ _ _   _ _ _ _ _ _ (a boy in a cartoon)
4 _ _ _   _ _ _ _ _ _   _ _ _ _ _ _ (a tennis player)
5 _ _ _ _ _   _ _ _ _ _ _ _ (a football player)
6 _ _ _ _ _ _ _   _ _ _ _ _ _ _ (an actress)
7 _ _ _ _ _ _ _   _ _ _ _ _ _ _ _ _ (a film director)

## Listening

4 🎧 Listen to Maria asking four teenagers about their best friends. Complete the information.

1  Matt
Best friend is ......*Jonny*......
How old is he? ....................
What do they do together? ....................

2  Elena
Best friend is ....................
When do they meet? ....................

3  Kelly-Anne
Best friend is ......*Vicky*......
Why is she special? ....................
How old is Kelly-Anne? ....................

4  Tom
Best friend is ....................
Where do they go together? ....................

5 🎧 Listen and write short answers to Maria's questions.

1 What's your best friend called?
2 Can you spell that?
3 How old is he or she?
4 When do you meet?
5 Where do you go together?
6 What do you do together?
7 Why is your friend special?

6 Now ask and answer questions 1–7 from exercise 5 in pairs. Use some of this language from the recording.

| asking | answering |
|---|---|
| OK ... | Well ... |
| Right ... | That's easy. |
| So ... | That's difficult. |
| And ... | That's right. |

# 1.2 Borrow this!

1 What things do you lend your friends? Do they always give them back? Use these words to help you.

> CDs    DVDs    money    clothes    make-up
> computer games    books    magazines

2 Read the photo story with another student. Why is Sam angry at the beginning? Why isn't he angry at the end?

**1** What's wrong, Sam? Are you sad or angry?

I'm angry. Gary's got six of my CDs!

**2** That's a lot! When do you want them back?

Now, but he doesn't want to give them back!

**3** Do you know about Gary's father? He isn't well.

Oh dear, I didn't know that. Is he very ill?

**4** He was in hospital last week but he's at home now.

That's good.

I know, let's invite Gary to the cinema. What can we go and see? Something funny, to make him laugh.

**5** Has Gary got your *Radiohead* CDs? I can lend you mine.

Don't worry. It doesn't really matter.

**6** OK. Are you free tonight, Sam?

Good idea, Lisa. How about sending him a text now?

**7** Yes. Why don't we meet at 7.30 at the cinema?

**8** Gary can come with us! I think he's pleased.

Great! Can you text him about my CDs?

# Grammar   Asking questions

3   Read the photo story again and find:
- six *Yes/No* questions
- three *Wh-* questions
- two suggestions

Look carefully at the order of the words. Then complete the grammar rules below.

### *Yes/No* questions in the present tense

- In questions with **have got**, the verb *have* always comes ...at the beginning... of the sentence and *got* comes ...after... the subject.

  EXAMPLE: Has Gary got your Radiohead CDs?

- In questions with **be**, the verb also comes .............................................. of the sentence.

  EXAMPLES: ..............................................
  ..............................................
  ..............................................

- In questions with **can**, the verb also comes .............................................. of the sentence.

  EXAMPLE: ..............................................

- With **other verbs**, we start the question with .............................. or *Does*. The main verb comes .............................. the subject.

  EXAMPLE: ..............................................

### *Wh-* questions in the present tense

- In questions with **be**, **have got** and **can**, the verb comes .............................. the question word.

  EXAMPLES: ..............................................
  ..............................................

- With **other verbs**, .............. or .............. comes after the question word. The subject comes next and the main verb comes .............. the subject.

  EXAMPLE: ..............................................

- **Suggestions**
  - We can use **Why don't/doesn't** and .............................................. to make suggestions.

  EXAMPLES: ..............................................
  ..............................................

G ···> page 135

4   Here are some errors that candidates have made with questions in the KET exam. Correct the questions. Two are correct.

1  When you want to come here?
2  Where you are now?
3  How about meet me at 7 o'clock?
4  Why don't we meet at the station?
5  Why you think it is interesting?
6  What do you want to buy?
7  How I can get there?
8  Who he does like?

5   Ask and answer questions about the photo story.

EXAMPLE: A: *Why is Sam angry?*
B: *Because Gary's got his CDs.*

# Vocabulary

6   Complete the sentences with an adjective from the box.

| angry | boring | free | funny | ~~ill~~ |
|-------|--------|------|-------|-----|
| pleased | sad | special | | |

1  My friend's ........ill........ at the moment – she's in bed with flu.
2  Your birthday is a very .................... day.
3  Are you .................... tonight? Do you want to go out?
4  The film was .................... and I fell asleep.
5  I'm really .................... to see you again!
6  Don't look so .................... – it isn't a true story.
7  Why is John ....................? Did you do something wrong?
8  Do you think this cartoon's ....................? It doesn't make me laugh.

## Activity

### Questionnaires

- Look at the questionnaire on page 128. Ask questions to complete the questionnaire about your partner. You can ask for difficult words to be spelled!

- Tell the class about your partner, using the questionnaire to help you.

# Exam folder 1

## Listening Part 1    Short conversations

In Part 1 of the Listening paper, you will hear some short conversations on different topics. There are always two speakers (usually a man and a woman). There are five questions and an example question. You must choose the correct answer from options A, B or C. These options can be pictures, words or numbers.

*Note:* Write your answers on the question paper during the test. **You do not transfer any answers to the answer sheet until the end of the test.**

Here is an example of the answer sheet for Part 1. You must write your answers in pencil.

| Part 1 | | | |
|---|---|---|---|
| 1 | A | B | C |
| 2 | A | B | C |
| 3 | A | B | C |
| 4 | A | B | C |
| 5 | A | B | C |

Here is an example question. Read the question and the recording script. Match the parts in colour to pictures A, B or C. Then look at the other words in the recording script and decide on the correct answer.

What did David do after school?

A                                    B                                    C

**Mother:**  You're late, David. Did you work in the library after your lessons finished?
**David:**   Mum, it was too sunny to be inside!  I watched the football team with some of my friends. They won the match! I can go to the library another afternoon.
**Mother:**  I suppose so. Well, why don't you go on the PlayStation with your sister before dinner?
**David:**   She's busy with her homework.

### Exam advice

*Before you listen*
- Read the questions and look at the choices to help you understand the topic.
- Underline the important words in each question.

*First listening*
- Listen out for the underlined words or words that are like these. In the example above, the word *school* is in the question, and the word *lessons* is on the recording.

- Remember to listen carefully for the tense (e.g. present simple, present perfect) and person (e.g. *he, she, they*) used in the question.
- Tick your answer in pencil on the question paper.

*Second listening*
- Check your choice of answer is correct and fill in any answers you didn't get the first time.

**Questions 1–5**

You will hear five short conversations.
You will hear each conversation twice.
There is one question for each conversation.
For questions **1–5**, put a tick (✓) under the right answer.

**1** What is the man buying for his lunch?

A ☐        B ☐        C ☐

**2** When is Maria's party?

A ☐        B ☐        C ☐

**3** Which postcard does the woman choose?

A ☐        B ☐        C ☐

**4** How much does the woman pay for the DVD?

£9.50        £10.50        £19.50

A ☐        B ☐        C ☐

**5** What did the girl leave at Ben's flat?

A ☐        B ☐        C ☐

# 2.1 For sale

## Vocabulary

1 Name the things in the photos. Where can you buy them?
Match each group of things to a place in the box.

> bookshop    chemist    department store
> market    newsagent

2 What else can you buy in each place? Make lists.

3 How much shopping do you do? Answer these
questions.

1 How much chocolate do you buy every week?
2 How many magazines do you get each
month?
3 How much money do you spend on sweets?
4 How many CDs do you have?
5 How many T-shirts did you buy last summer?

GRAMMAR EXTRA

**How much ...? How many ...?**

- We ask *How much ...?* with uncountable
  nouns (e.g. *shopping, chocolate, money*).

- We ask *How many ...?* with countable nouns
  (e.g. *magazines, CDs, T-shirts*).

4 Ask and answer questions using *How much ...?*
or *How many ...?* with these nouns.

> books    DVDs    make-up    shampoo
> clothes    toothpaste    shoes

# Reading

5 Look quickly at texts A–H. Where can you see them?

EXAMPLE: *You can see A on a sweater.*

6 Read the texts more carefully. What letters are missing?

A
ND WASH IN COLD WATER

B
P
rking is free for customers

C
de of 100% leather

D
sta dishes all £4.95 with
lad & mineral water

E
RROTS
60P/ KILO

F
TURDAY 5 SEPT, 21.00
CKETS £15 & £20

G
MERAS HALF PRICE –
LE ENDS TOMORROW!

H
VERT:
mes for PlayStation
ly £7 each
one: 01956 823001

7 Which text (A–H) says this (1–5)?

1 Things are cheaper than usual today.
2 You get a drink with this meal.
3 Call the number if you are interested in any of these.
4 It costs nothing to leave your car if you are shopping here.
5 Do not put this in a machine.

## Pronunciation

8 🎧 Listen and repeat. Underline the letters that make the sounds /ɑː/, /eɪ/ and /æ/.

/ɑː/
car
supermarket
artist
department store

/eɪ/
whale
sale
PlayStation
email

/æ/
apple
map
carrot
advert

9 Look at exercise 6 again and find more words for the three lists in exercise 8. Say them first and then write them down.

1 What are these ways of shopping? Do you do any shopping like this? Is it better than going into shops? Why? / Why not?

## Listening

2 Read the conversation. Don't worry about the spaces at the moment. What is the conversation about?

**Kevin:** Good morning. Swimshop, Kevin speaking. How can I help you?

**Sally:** Hello. I've got your catalogue here and I'd like some information. Can you give me some prices?

**Kevin:** Of course. Please tell me the page number you're looking at.

**Sally:** OK. The first thing is on page (**1**) ........ and it's the Maru swimming costume, the blue and green one.

**Kevin:** OK, the small and medium sizes are £22.65 and the large one is (**2**) £ ...... .

**Sally:** Right. I'd like to order that, please, size small.

**Kevin:** Fine. Have you got any more things to order?

**Sally:** Yes, I'd like some pool shoes for water sports. They're on page (**3**) ........ . How much are the blue and yellow ones?

**Kevin:** Well, they were £16.50 but they're in the sale now and they're only (**4**) £ ........ . But we don't have any left in small sizes. What shoe size are you?

**Sally:** I'm a (**5**) ........ .

**Kevin:** Let me check. Yes, we've got a pair in that size.

**Sally:** Great. Well, that's all I need. My name and address is ...

3 🎧 Now listen to the conversation and write the missing numbers.

## Grammar  *some* and *any*

**4** Look at these sentences from page 16.

1 I'd like some pool shoes.
2 I'd like some information.
3 Have you got any more things to order?
4 We don't have any left in small sizes.
5 Can you give me some prices?

Complete rules a–e with *some* or *any* and match them to 1–5.

**a** We use ......*some*...... with uncountable nouns in affirmative sentences. ☑2

**b** We always use ...................... in negative sentences. ☐

**c** We use ...................... with countable nouns in affirmative sentences. ☐

**d** We use ...................... for a request. ☐

**e** We usually use ...................... in questions. ☐

**G** ⋯⟫ page 136

**G** ⋯⟫ page 136

### SPELLING SPOT
**Plurals**

Countable nouns usually have different singular and plural forms, e.g. *car, cars.*

With uncountable nouns, there is only one form of the word, e.g. *toothpaste.*

- To make a plural, we usually add *-s:*
  *one book     some books*

- When the noun ends in *-sh, -ch, -ss, -s* or *-x*, we add *-es:*

  | | |
  |---|---|
  | *dish* | *dishes* |
  | *sandwich* | *sandwiches* |
  | *glass* | *glasses* |
  | *bus* | *buses* |
  | *box* | *boxes* |

- When the noun ends in *-o* after a consonant, we also add *-es:*

  | | |
  |---|---|
  | *tomato* | *tomatoes* |
  | *potato* | *potatoes* |

- When the noun ends in *-y* after a **vowel**, we add *-s:*

  | | |
  |---|---|
  | *toy* | *toys* |

- When the noun ends in *-y* after a **consonant**, we change *y* to *i* and add *-es:*

  | | |
  |---|---|
  | *story* | *stories* |

- Some nouns have irregular plurals, for example:

  | | |
  |---|---|
  | *woman* | *women* |
  | *child* | *children* |
  | *fish* | *fish* |
  | *foot* | *feet* |

**5** Complete the sentences with *some* or *any.*

1 I can't find ......*any*...... sunglasses I like here.
2 There are ...................... nice jackets in the shops at the moment.
3 Are there ...................... yellow surfing T-shirts in the sale?
4 I want to buy ...................... trainers, please.
5 Mum, can you lend me ...................... money?
6 There's ...................... great make-up in this advert.
7 Has that website got ...................... special prices?
8 Why don't we buy ...................... new DVDs?
9 There isn't ...................... bread left – can you get ...................... in town?
10 Let's buy ...................... new glasses.

### Activity

**Picture puzzle**

- Look at the pictures. Write the singular and plural forms of the word under each picture.

1 ......*cat*......
......*cats*......
2 ......................
......................
3 ......................
......................
4 ......................
......................
5 ......................
......................
6 ......................
......................
7 ......................
......................
8 ......................
......................
9 ......................
......................
10 ......................
......................
11 ......................
......................
12 ......................
......................
13 ......................
......................
14 ......................
......................

- Then write the last letter of each singular form in the boxes below. They make three words. What do the words say?

| 1 | 2 | 3 | 4 | 5 | 6 | 7 | 8 | 9 | 10 | 11 | 12 | 13 | 14 |
|---|---|---|---|---|---|---|---|---|----|----|----|----|----|
| t | | | | | | | | | | | | | |

# Exam folder 2

## Reading Part 1    Notices

Part 1 of the Reading and Writing paper is a matching task. There are five questions and an example question. You must choose the correct answer from eight notices (A–H).

1   These language areas are often tested in Part 1. Add another example to each one.

   1  modal verbs  *You can*
   2  comparison  *older*
   3  imperatives  *Don't forget*
   4  prepositions with times and days of the week  *until 5 pm*
   5  prepositions with places  *next to the restaurant*

2   Decide what sort of language is tested in the exam task above.
    Underline examples of language areas 1–5 above in different colours.

### Exam advice

- Look at the eight notices first to see what the topics are.
- Read the example and its notice.
- Cross out the example letter, so that you don't choose it again by accident.
- Read each sentence carefully and underline the key words.
- Look for notices that have similar language.
- Don't just match a word or number in the sentence and notice – this may not be the right answer.
- Check your answers when you transfer them to your answer sheet. Below is an example of the answer sheet for Part 1.

| Part 1 | | | | | | | | |
|---|---|---|---|---|---|---|---|---|
| **1** | A | B | C | D | E | F | G | H |
| **2** | A | B | C | D | E | F | G | H |
| **3** | A | B | C | D | E | F | G | H |
| **4** | A | B | C | D | E | F | G | H |
| **5** | A | B | C | D | E | F | G | H |

## Part 1

Questions 1–5

Which notice (**A–H**) says this (**1–5**)?

For questions **1–5**, mark the correct letter **A–H** on your answer sheet.

**Example:**

**0**  Do not leave any suitcases on the floor.    *Answer:*  | 0 | A B C D E F G H |

---

**1**  It is possible to swim later in the evening now.

**A**  Buy train tickets at machine when office is closed

**2**  This is cheaper because it isn't new.

**B**  FOR SALE
Boy's bike, only 2 months old
Half usual price

**3**  All our prices are lower for a short time.

**C**  TICKETS FOR TONIGHT'S CONCERT ARE ON SALE HERE FROM 7 PM

**4**  You can pay for your journey in a different way if necessary.

**D**  PLEASE PUT ALL LUGGAGE ABOVE YOUR SEAT

**5**  If you are 15 or younger, you may win some money.

**E**  SALE ENDS NEXT TUESDAY – 15% OFF EVERYTHING UNTIL THEN

**F**  UNDER 16s GOLF COMPETITION **FIRST PRIZE £30!**

**G**  SPEND £50 AND GET A **FREE** SPORTS BAG

**H**  POOL OPENING HOURS NOW LONGER: 7 am – 10 pm (was 8.45 pm)

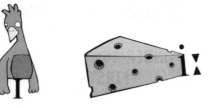

1 Look at the photos. Tell your partner what you see, then complete the puzzle below to find the word in the yellow squares.

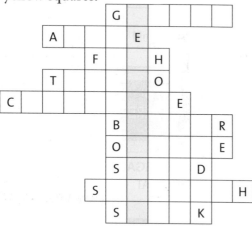

## Listening

3 🎧 Listen to Jack and Katie talking about food and drink. Write J for Jack and K for Katie. Who …

1 always has a big breakfast? J
2 buys a cake for a snack?
3 has chips or pizza for lunch?
4 thinks salad is good for you?
5 prefers water to juice?
6 doesn't like coffee or tea?
7 loves chocolate?
8 doesn't like ice cream?

## Pronunciation

2 🎧 Listen and repeat these words. Then write them in group 1 or group 2 below.

| meal | fish | leave | meat | fill | biscuit | bin | tea |
|------|------|-------|------|------|---------|-----|-----|
| chips | eat | feel | seat | dinner | sit | live | beans |

| group 1 /ɪ/ chicken | group 2 /iː/ cheese |
|---------------------|---------------------|
|                     |                     |

🎧 Listen to the recording to check your answers.

# Vocabulary

4 What do you like? What don't you like? Talk about the food and drink in 1–7.

EXAMPLE:
*I like apples best. / I prefer apples.*
*I quite like oranges.*
*Grapes are OK.*
*I hate bananas.*

| 1 apples | grapes | bananas | oranges |
|---|---|---|---|
| 2 potatoes | rice | pasta | bread |
| 3 steak | chicken | fish | cheese |
| 4 pizza | sandwiches | burgers | soup |
| 5 ice cream | cake | biscuits | chocolate |
| 6 lemonade | juice | water | coffee |
| 7 salad | carrots | onions | tomatoes |

5 Find out what four people in your class like and don't like. Write down their answers.

EXAMPLE: Ask:  *What do you like?*
Write: *Sergio likes steak best and he doesn't like fish.*

## Grammar  Present simple

6 Complete this table with *like*.

| affirmative | I/You/We/They | ........................... chocolate. |
| | He/She/It | ........................... bananas. |
| negative | I/You/We/They | ........................... fish. |
| | He/She/It | ........................... oranges. |
| question | ................ I/you/we/they .............. apples? | |
| | ................ he/she/it ................... burgers? | |

G ⟶ page 136

7 Match the times with the clocks.

a (clock) b (clock) c (clock) d (clock)

1 seven forty-five; a quarter to eight
2 one forty-two; eighteen minutes to two
3 four o'clock
4 two fifteen; a quarter past two
5 eight minutes past three
6 five thirty; half past five

e (clock)

f (clock)

8 Read the questions below. Which answers are correct? Put a tick next to them.

Excuse me, can you tell me the time, please?
or
Have you got the time, please?

A Yes, of course. It's six o'clock.
B No, I don't.
C It's too early.
D No, I'm sorry. I don't have a watch.
E Nine minutes past three.
F Certainly, a quarter to four.
G I'm not sure.

### SPELLING SPOT
#### Contractions

9 Complete the table.

| does + not = | *doesn't* |
| do + not = | *don't* |
| has + not = | .................... |
| have + not = | .................... |
| is + not = | .................... |
| are + not = | .................... |

10 🎧 Listen to Rachel talking about her day. Complete the notes.

**Breakfast – 8.00 am**
tea
(1) ....................................
toast

**Lunch – (2)** ................... pm
salad
a cake
(3) ....................................

**Dinner – (4)** ................... pm
chicken or (5) ...................
rice or pasta
(6) ....................................

Tell your partner about your day.

# 3.2 Food at festivals

1 What can you see in the photo?

## Reading

2 Read the text below about a festival in Spain.

Antonio lives in the city of Valencia in Spain. Every year he goes to La Tomatina Festival in Buñol, a town near Valencia. The festival is on the last Wednesday in August, when everyone comes into the main square to throw tomatoes at each other.

Before the fun begins, people cover the shop windows with plastic. Antonio always wears his oldest clothes so he doesn't get his best clothes dirty. He also always puts his camera in a plastic bag to keep it clean. In the morning trucks arrive in the main square, the Plaza del Pueblo, bringing more than 100,000 kilos of tomatoes. The fight begins at 11 o'clock and always lasts for two hours. At exactly 1 o'clock everyone stops. They never throw tomatoes after 1 o'clock. They then usually spend the rest of the day cleaning themselves and the town! In the evening, Antonio usually watches the fireworks, eats the local food and sometimes joins in the dancing.

Are these sentences right or wrong? Underline the part of the text with the answer in.

1 Antonio comes from Buñol.
2 The festival is at the beginning of August.
3 Antonio never wears his best clothes to the festival.
4 Everyone buys tomatoes from a local shop.
5 The fight usually lasts for more than two hours.
6 The next day everyone cleans the streets.
7 Antonio always watches the fireworks.
8 Antonio sometimes dances.

## GRAMMAR EXTRA — Adverbs of frequency

| always | 100% |
| usually | |
| She often has a special meal on her birthday. | |
| sometimes | |
| never | 0% |

Adverbs of frequency come …

- before most verbs: He **always** goes to the festival.
- after the verb be: I am **always** late for dinner.
- *Sometimes* can also be placed at the beginning or end of the sentence: I am **sometimes** late for school. **Sometimes** I am late for school. I am late for school **sometimes**.

3 Complete these sentences with *always, often, usually, sometimes* or *never*.

1 I get up at 9 o'clock. (100%)
   *I always get up at 9 o'clock.*
2 My mother makes cakes on Tuesdays. (75%)
3 I am hungry at lunch time. (100%)
4 I am late for dinner. (55%)
5 Pete has a party on his birthday. (100%)
6 We have fireworks on New Year's Eve. (25%)
7 Sam meets his friends on New Year's Eve. (90%)
8 You eat spaghetti with a knife. (0%)

## Reading

4 Read about New Year in Japan. Fill each space with one of the verbs from the box in the correct form. Two of the verbs are negative.

| stay | begin | eat (x 2) | go (x 3) | ~~come~~ |
| clean | send | watch | listen | drink |
| ring | enjoy | make | receive | do |

Akiko Imai (1) ....*comes*.... from Japan. Many young Japanese people often (2) ........................ away with their friends at New Year but Akiko (3) ........................ usually ........................ away, she (4) ........................ at home with her family. In Japan, New Year (5) ........................ on 31st December. On that day, Akiko (6) ........................ TV and (7) ........................ a special kind of pasta called soba. At midnight (12 o'clock), she (8) ........................ to the sound of the temple bell ringing. It (9) ........................ 108 times. On New Year's Day, 1st January, Akiko and her family (10) ........................ sake, a kind of rice wine. After, they all (11) ........................ popular foods like rice cake and soup. It is a special day for children because they (12) ........................ some money in special envelopes from their relatives. Before New Year's Day, Japanese people usually (13) ........................ their houses, (14) ........................ a lot of food and (15) ........................ a lot of shopping. Akiko often (16) ........................ greetings cards to her friends. New Year is one of the most important days in Japan and Akiko always (17) ........................ it because she (18) ........................ to school on that day!

5 Tell your partner about your special days.

> What do you do at New Year?

> We often have fireworks.

> What do you do on public holidays?

> I usually go to a restaurant.

> What happens when there is a festival in your town?

6 Write a note to a friend about a festival in your town.

Say:
- when the festival is
- what you do at the festival
- what you eat.

### Activity

**When's your birthday?**

- Form groups of four to six students.
- Then everyone in the group must stand in the order of the date of their birthday.
- The winners are the team who get in the right order first. Everyone must be able to say the date of their birthday in English. If you can't, your team is out.

# Writing folder 1

## Writing Part 6
## Spelling words

In Part 6 of the Reading and Writing paper there are five questions (**36–40**) and an example. Each question is a sentence which gives a description of a word. You must write the word, spelling it correctly. The first letter of the word is always given to you.

Here are some ways to practise spelling.

1   Match the first part of the word in A to the second part in B. The words are all about food and drink.

EXAMPLE: *meat*

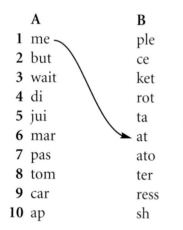

| A | B |
|---|---|
| 1 me | ple |
| 2 but | ce |
| 3 wait | ket |
| 4 di | rot |
| 5 jui | ta |
| 6 mar | at |
| 7 pas | ato |
| 8 tom | ter |
| 9 car | ress |
| 10 ap | sh |

2   KET students often find some words difficult to spell. Find the word which is spelled wrongly in each group and correct the spelling.

| | | | | |
|---|---|---|---|---|
| 1 favourite | (diferent) | disappointed | traditional | *different* |
| 2 actor | nurse | painter | pilat | |
| 3 pink | white | yello | grey | |
| 4 bath | chair | bed | mirrer | |
| 5 husband | mother | daughter | unkle | |
| 6 beatiful | famous | rich | single | |
| 7 television | telefone | cooker | camera | |
| 8 cloudy | sunney | stormy | windy | |
| 9 wich | who | that | when | |
| 10 nice | friendly | confortable | interesting | |
| 11 hope | know | think | belive | |
| 12 hospital | airport | library | appartment | |

3   Write a description for these words.

1   a dining room   *I eat in this room.* .........................

2   pizza   .............................................................

3   a waiter   .........................................................

4   a café   ...........................................................

5   breakfast   .......................................................

6   a snack   .........................................................

7   a kitchen   .......................................................

8   a fridge   .........................................................

9   fruit   .............................................................

10  ice cream   ......................................................

4   Think of your own descriptions and ask your partner what the answer is.

EXAMPLE: A: *This is brown and it's very sweet. What is it?*
               B: *Chocolate.*

## Exam advice

- Read each sentence carefully.
- Count the number of spaces to find out how many letters the word has.
- Decide if the word needs to be plural or not (look for words like *this* or *these*).
- Write your answer on the question paper first.
- Check you have used the right number of letters.
- Write your answer on your answer sheet. Opposite is an example of the answer sheet for Part 6.

| Part 6 | | Do not write here |
|---|---|---|
| 36 | | 1 ▢ 36 2 ▢ |
| 37 | | 1 ▢ 37 2 ▢ |
| 38 | | 1 ▢ 38 2 ▢ |
| 39 | | 1 ▢ 39 2 ▢ |
| 40 | | 1 ▢ 40 2 ▢ |

## Part 6

### Questions 36–40

Read the descriptions (**36–40**) of some things you can eat or drink.
What is the word for each one?
The first letter is already there. There is one space for each other letter in the word.

For questions **36–40**, write the words on your answer sheet.

**Example:**

**0** This is a popular fast food and you eat it in a bun.  b _ _ _ _ _

*Answer:*  | **0** | burger |

---

**36** It is good to drink this when the weather is hot.  l _ _ _ _ _ _ _

**37** These are red and you find them on pizza.  t _ _ _ _ _ _ _

**38** This fruit is round and has lots of juice.  o _ _ _ _ _

**39** This makes food sweet.  s _ _ _ _

**40** You often eat these on a picnic.  s _ _ _ _ _ _ _ _

# 4.1 A long journey

1 Match the people below with their nationality. What are they famous for doing?

Roald Amundsen
Ferdinand Magellan
Ranulph Fiennes
Neil Armstrong
Hernán Cortés
Marco Polo

American
British
Spanish
Portuguese
Italian
Norwegian

1 Where did the Polo family come from? They were a rich family and they lived in Italy over 750 years ago. They travelled all over the Mediterranean. They bought and sold things like gold and silver. Marco was born in 1254 in Venice.

## Reading

2 Marco was only six years old when his father and uncle went on their first journey to China. In China, they met the King of the Mongols, Kublai Khan.

3 Marco didn't see his father again for nine years. He was 15 when his father and uncle returned from China. The next time his father and uncle decided to go to China they took Marco with them. This was in 1271.
They went by ship to Turkey and then used horses.
It was a long journey.

4 In 1275 they arrived in Khanbalik (modern Beijing) and saw Kublai Khan. He talked to them and asked them many questions. He liked Marco and so he gave him a job. What did Marco do in China? Well, he travelled all over the country. He saw that the Chinese used paper money and used a machine to print books.

5 He visited the largest city in China, called Kinsai, many times. He said that the people in Kinsai wore beautiful clothes and ate good food. There were ten big markets in Kinsai and they sold everything people wanted.

6 Marco stayed in China for 17 years. The journey home took Marco and his family two years. In Italy, Marco decided to write a book about his life in China. Many people didn't believe Marco's stories at first. Later, they believed him. Marco died in 1324.

VENICE
KINSAI

2 Read the information about Marco Polo. Are the sentences opposite right or wrong? If there is no information, write 'Doesn't say'.

EXAMPLES:
Marco Polo lived over 850 years ago.
*Wrong. He didn't live 850 years ago, he lived 750 years ago.*
Marco travelled all over the Mediterranean.
*Doesn't say.*
Marco came from Venice.
*Right.*

1 Marco first went to China when he was six years old.
2 It took Marco and his family a long time to get to China.
3 Marco travelled to China by boat and on a horse.
4 Marco spoke to Kublai Khan.
5 Marco liked Kublai Khan very much.
6 Kinsai had twelve markets.
7 Marco took a long time to write his book about China.
8 Marco died a poor man.

## Grammar  Past simple

3  Look at paragraph 1 in the story about Marco Polo. Find the past simple form of these verbs.

*regular verbs*
1 live    ..............................
2 travel  ..............................

*irregular verbs*
3 buy     ..............................
4 sell    ..............................
5 be      .............................. (two forms)

Now complete these sentences.

**Making a question:**
Where .................. the Polo family .................. from?
**Making a negative:**
Many people .................. .................. Marco's stories at first.

**G** ···⟫ page 137

---

**SPELLING SP T**

### Regular verbs in the past simple

Regular verbs in the past simple end in -ed.

- If the verb ends in -e, e.g. *decide*
  ▶ add -d  *They decided to go to China.*
- If the verb ends in a consonant + vowel + consonant, e.g. *travel*
  ▶ double the last letter and add -ed
    *They travelled all over the Mediterranean.*
- If the verb ends in a consonant + -y, e.g. *study*
  ▶ -y becomes -ied  *He studied the country carefully.*
- If the verb ends in vowel + -y, e.g. *stay*
  ▶ add -ed  *He stayed there for 17 years.*
- If the verb ends in two or more consonants, e.g. *ask*
  ▶ add -ed  *He asked them many questions.*

4  What is the past simple of the following verbs?

| | | |
|---|---|---|
| 1 arrive | 5 use | 9 carry |
| 2 stop | 6 return | 10 open |
| 3 help | 7 like | |
| 4 look | 8 play | |

---

## Pronunciation

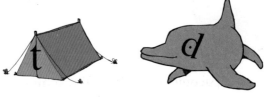

5  There are three ways to pronounce a regular verb in the past simple: /t/, /d/ and /ɪd/. Underline all the regular verbs in the story about Marco Polo and decide which column, /t/, /d/ or /ɪd/, to put them in.

| /t/ | /d/ | /ɪd/ |
|---|---|---|
| | | |
| | | |
| | | |
| | | |

🎧 Listen to the recording to check your answers.

6  Read the Marco Polo story again to find the past simple of these irregular verbs. (You can find more irregular verbs on page 151.)

| | | |
|---|---|---|
| 1 wear | 5 meet | 9 buy |
| 2 give | 6 take | 10 see |
| 3 eat | 7 say | |
| 4 sell | 8 go | |

### Activity

**Who is it?**

- 🎧 Listen to two students playing *Who is it?* Who is the famous person?
- Now, you play. Player A thinks of a famous person from the past. Player B asks up to twelve questions to find out the name of the person.

EXAMPLE: B: *Were you a man?*
         A: *Yes, I was. / No, I wasn't.*
         B: *Did you paint pictures?*
         A: *No, I didn't. / Yes, I did.*

# 4.2 A trip to remember

1 Ask your partner questions about an interesting place he or she visited last year.

EXAMPLE: Where / go?

A: *Where did you go?*

B: *I went to an art gallery / to a museum / to London.*

When / go?          How much / cost?
How / travel?       What / see?
What / do?          How long / stay?
Who / go with?

## Listening

2 🎧 Listen to a girl called Melanie talking about a school trip to Paris. Circle the correct answer.

1 Number of days in Paris: *2 / 5*
2 Coach left school at: *5.00 / 5.30* am
3 Cost of trip: *£240 / £214*
4 Name of hotel in Paris: *BERRI / VERRY*
5 Enjoyed *shopping / boat trip* best.

3 🎧 Now listen to Melanie again and answer with short answers.

1 Did the students arrive at school late?
*No, they didn't.*
2 Did Melanie like the coach journey?
3 Did they stop at a café on the motorway for some sandwiches?
4 Did it take eight hours to go from London to Paris?
5 Did they stay at a new hotel?
6 Did Melanie speak French all the time?
7 Did Melanie buy a present for her sister?
8 Did she take lots of photos?
9 Did she enjoy the trip?
10 Did they arrive back in London late?

**Past simple + *ago***

> *When did Melanie go on the school trip to Paris?*
> *Two years* **ago**.
> *When did you last see a film?*
> *A week* **ago**.

**4** Ask and answer with a partner. Answer using *ago* or one of the expressions in the box below.

EXAMPLE: brush teeth
A: *When did you last brush your hair?*
B: *I brushed my hair two weeks ago.*

last night/week/Saturday/month/year
this morning/afternoon
yesterday
in the summer/winter/spring/autumn
at breakfast/lunch/dinner time
at the weekend

1 eat some chocolate
2 email a friend
3 read a magazine
4 listen to a CD
5 go to the cinema
6 play football
7 do some homework
8 go to an art gallery
9 buy some clothes
10 eat pizza

I brushed my hair two weeks ago.

**5** Here are some errors that candidates have made with the past simple in the KET exam. Correct the sentences. There is one correct sentence.

1 Yesterday I go to the disco.
2 Who you went to an art gallery with?
3 Last night I have a good dinner and saw a film.
4 Last year I went to New York and it is very interesting.
5 I plaied football with my brother on Saturday.
6 Tomas came to England in two years ago.
7 Why you not came to see me?
8 Angela visited a museum two weeks ago.
9 How much costed the trip?
10 Shakespeare writing many plays.

## Activity

### Word Puzzle

- Find ten verbs in the past simple in the word square (look ↓ , →). The first one has been done for you.

| l | l | q | u | b | s | d | e | t | s |
|---|---|---|---|---|---|---|---|---|---|
| i | d | w | t | a | t | a | t | e | t |
| k | d | w | a | t | k | r | y | u | a |
| e | s | e | r | o | j | r | j | k | y |
| d | a | n | g | o | k | l | s | w | e |
| m | b | t | f | k | t | v | a | d | d |
| p | u | i | h | f | c | e | w | i | c |
| b | e | g | a | n | s | d | r | v | x |
| o | z | a | d | p | d | a | t | u | i |
| l | t | r | a | v | e | l | l | e | d |

- Use five of the verbs you found in a short paragraph about a trip you made.

## Speaking

1 Read these sentences with a partner. Say if each sentence is true for you and give some extra information.

EXAMPLE: My friends like the same things as I do.
*No, not true. My friends are all very different. My best friend likes listening to bands. Some of my other friends like skateboarding and one prefers to play on his computer.*

1 I had a great party for my birthday.
2 I prefer to have a lot of friends, not just one best friend.
3 I spend a lot of money on CDs and DVDs.
4 I don't care about fashion.
5 I love chocolate.
6 I think people eat too much nowadays.
7 My best friend never makes me angry.
8 I like going on trips with my parents more than I do with my school.

## Vocabulary

2 Circle the odd one out.

| | | | |
|---|---|---|---|
| 1 sad | happy | pleased | (green) |
| 2 nice | short | boring | funny |
| 3 interesting | boring | friend | exciting |
| 4 shop | store | house | market |
| 5 fish | meat | coffee | biscuits |
| 6 onion | orange | apple | lemon |
| 7 café | dining room | restaurant | hall |
| 8 art gallery | museum | exhibition | bookshop |

3 Put the letters in the right order to spell things you can eat and drink.

1 l e v a b e g e t
2 c k a n s
3 t e a m
4 k l m i
5 c e j i u
6 p e g a r
7 s h f i
8 r r c t a o
9 t b t r e u
10 o c o h l t a c e
11 o t p a o t
12 n c e k h i c

## Writing

4 Read the descriptions of different places where you can buy things. What is the word for each one? The first letter is already there.

1 People can buy fruit and vegetables here.
m _ _ _ _ _

2 This shop sells newspapers.
n _ _ _ _ _ _ _ _

3 This shop sells medicines.
c _ _ _ _ _ _

4 If you go here, you can buy most things.
s _ _ _ _ _ _ _ _ _ _

5 Buy your stamps at this place.
p _ _ _ o _ _ _ _ _

# Grammar

## 5 Circle the correct word.

1 Can I have *any* / (*some*) cake, please?

2 How *much* / *many* money do you have in your pocket?

3 How much *is* / *are* the blue pair of trainers?

4 I haven't got *any* / *some* change.

5 *Does* / *Do* he like eating at restaurants?

6 Can you *say* / *tell* me the time, please?

7 Have you got *any* / *the* time, please?

8 *Sometimes* / *Always* I go to a party on New Year's Eve.

9 Lisa *doesn't* / *don't* make a special cake for her birthday.

10 I didn't *went* / *go* shopping at the weekend.

11 *Did* / *Have* Marco Polo travel to Persia?

12 When did he *return* / *returned* to Venice?

## 6 Write the past simple of these irregular verbs.

1 know
2 forget
3 say
4 sell
5 teach
6 tell
7 wear
8 leave
9 grow
10 think

## 7 Read this conversation and put the verbs into the correct tense.

**Jenny:** Hi Sam! How (**1**) ....*are*.... (be) you?

**Sam:** I (**2**) .............. (be) fine, thanks, Jenny. I (**3**) .............. (telephone) you yesterday. Where (**4**) .............. (be) you?

**Jenny:** I (**5**) .............. (need) some new shoes so I (**6**) .............. (go) shopping in town.

**Sam:** (**7**) .............. (you / get) any?

**Jenny:** Yes, look. What (**8**) .............. (you / think) of them?

**Sam:** Oh, I (**9**) .............. (not be) sure that I (**10**) .............. (like) the colour. (**11**) .............. (be) they blue?

**Jenny:** No, they (**12**) .............. (be) green! I (**13**) .............. (think) at first they (**14**) .............. (be) blue as well, but when I (**15**) .............. (take) them outside the shop I (**16**) .............. (see) that they (**17**) .............. (be) green.

**Sam:** (**18**) .............. (be) they expensive? They (**19**) .............. (look) very expensive to me.

**Jenny:** No, I (**20**) .............. (get) them in the sale.

## 8 Read this article about Chinese New Year. Choose the correct word for 1–10.

Chinese New Year (1) *starts* / *start* with the New Moon on the first day of the New Year and ends on the full moon 15 days later. Chinese New Year is on a different date (2) *each* / *a* year. New Year's Eve and New Year's Day are when families celebrate together. People (3) *make* / *makes* large amounts of food for (4) *his* / *their* family and friends. On New Year's Day they (5) *ate* / *eat* a dish of vegetables, called jai. Other foods include a whole fish, chicken and noodles. In South China, for (6) *some* / *any* people the favourite dish is sweet rice.

People clean their houses before New Year's Day. On New Year's Eve there are fireworks and (7) *at* / *on* midnight everyone opens every door and window in their house to say goodbye to the old year. (8) *Many* / *Much* people (9) *wear* / *wearing* red clothes at New Year because it (10) *is* / *has* lucky. Children are given little red envelopes with money inside.

## Vocabulary

1  Put the letters in the right order to spell the names of the animals in the pictures above.

1  r e a b
2  e h s o r
3  a c t
4  g d o
5  e p a l e h n t
6  n o l d p i h
7  s h i f
8  r e d i p s
9  e y m k o n
10  w o c

2  What's your favourite animal? Have you got a pet? What's its name?

## Pronunciation

3  🎧 Listen to a man talking about the animals he likes.

*I like horses, cows, dogs and cats.*

*I like monkeys, elephants and bears.*

Ask five people in the class which animals they like and report back to the class.

EXAMPLE: *Pietro likes bears, dolphins and dogs.*

### GRAMMAR EXTRA
*and*

- After a verb we usually put *and* between the last two nouns, adjectives or verbs in a list, and commas (,) between the other things.

  *I like horses, cows, dogs **and** cats.*
  *The bear was large, hungry **and** dangerous.*
  *We swam, played volleyball **and** ate ice cream.*

- *And* is less common with adjectives before a noun. We normally just use a comma.

  *a big, yellow fish*

- When we use *and* we often miss out words instead of repeating them.

  *Nicole goes shopping **and** ~~she goes~~ swimming at the weekend.*
  *The monkeys **and** ~~the~~ birds were up in the trees.*

4  Here are some errors that candidates have made with *and* in the KET exam. Correct the sentences.

1  I saw a nice and colourful parrot at the zoo.
2  Yesterday we went to the zoo and yesterday we went to the museum.
3  Susanna went out yesterday and Susanna took her dog for a walk.
4  There are many cats, dogs, horses at the farm.
5  The dolphins were near the boat and the birds were near the boat.

## Listening

5 🎧 Listen to Mark talking to Natalie about visiting the zoo. Tick the word when you hear it. The words are not in the order you hear them.

1 zoo ✓    6 weekend
2 friend    7 camera
3 bus    8 Sunday
4 homework    9 four
5 student    10 drive

6 🎧 Look at the example and then listen to the first part of the conversation again.

EXAMPLE:
When will Mark and Natalie go to the zoo?
A Saturday
B Sunday
C Thursday

The answer is **C**. Natalie is busy on Saturday and Sunday.

🎧 Read through the questions and then listen to the rest of the conversation and answer the questions.

1 Each zoo ticket will cost them
  A £6.50.
  B £7.50.
  C £8.00.

2 Who is Mark going to take photos for?
  A his mother
  B his friend
  C his teacher

3 Mark is going to photograph
  A bears.
  B monkeys.
  C lions.

4 How will Mark and Natalie get to the zoo?
  A by bus
  B by train
  C by car

5 The zoo closes at
  A 4.30.
  B 5.30.
  C 6.30.

## Vocabulary

7 There are many words in English that go together. For example: *I've got to take some photographs of the animals.*

Put the words below in the right column. Sometimes there is more than one answer. Use and English–English dictionary to help you.

homework    time    a phone call
the shopping    an appointment    a cake
nothing    some money    an exam    breakfast

| do | make | take | spend |
|---|---|---|---|
|  |  | photographs |  |

8 Circle the correct word in these sentences about Mark and Natalie.

1 Natalie *made* / *spent* some time looking at the penguins.
2 Natalie *did* / *made* her homework when she got home from the zoo.
3 Mark *did* / *took* some shopping for his mum the next day.
4 Natalie said, 'Can you wait a minute? I need to *make* / *do* a phone call.'
5 Mark *took* / *made* his exams last week.
6 Natalie *did* / *made* a cake the next day.

9 Ask and answer these questions.

1 When do you do your homework?
2 Do you know how to make a cake?
3 Do you ever do nothing all day?
4 How much money do you spend on magazines?
5 How much time do you spend on the phone each day?
6 Do you help to do the food shopping at home?
7 Do you ever make dinner for your family?

1 Do this quiz with a partner before you read the article about polar bears.

1 Polar bears live in
 a) the Arctic.
 b) Antarctica.

2 Polar bears have
 a) white skin.
 b) black skin.

3 Polar bears usually eat
 a) fish.
 b) people.

4 Polar bears are about
 a) three metres long.
 b) six metres long.

5 Polar bears are the size of
 a) a car.
 b) a bus.

6 Polar bears usually have
 a) one baby.
 b) two babies.

7 Polar bears have their cubs every
 a) two years.
 b) three years.

8 Polar bears usually live
 a) in family groups.
 b) alone.

9 Polar bears are
 a) in danger.
 b) not in danger.

## Reading

2 Read the article to see if you were right. Don't worry about the spaces for now.

## Grammar Conjunctions

3 Look at the underlined words in paragraphs 1 and 2 in the article about the polar bear. Then complete the grammar explanation.

- We use _because_, .........., ..........
 and .......... to join two clauses to make one longer sentence.

 1 We use ..................... to say 'why' things happen.
 2 We use ..................... when there is a choice or an alternative fact or idea.
 3 We use ..................... when we want to add one fact or idea to another.
 4 We use ..................... when there is a contrast between the two facts or ideas.

**G** ···⟶ page 138

# In danger

The polar bear's name in Latin is *Ursus maritimus*, meaning 'sea bear'. It got this name <u>because</u> it spends most of its time in the Arctic seas. It is also called by other names, for example, white bear or ice bear. When a polar bear gets out of the sea, it shakes water from its fur like a dog <u>or</u> it removes the water by rolling on the ice. It is very cold where polar bears live. The temperature is very often as low as –55°C.

The polar bear is the largest meat-eating animal on land. The male weighs from 350 to 650 kg <u>and</u> he is two and a half to three metres long – almost as long as a car. A polar bear's skin is black <u>but</u> its fur has no colour – it looks white when the sun shines on the ice. It has big feet so it can stand easily on the ice.

The polar bear likes to live alone. It walks long distances, sometimes 30 km a day, (**1**) ........... it needs to find food. The bear eats fish (**2**) ........... it also enjoys seal meat. It goes swimming (**3**) ........... lies in the sun when it isn't looking for food! It is a very good swimmer.

The female bear usually has two babies once every three years. The babies, or cubs, are born in November. Sometimes the cubs die in their first year (**4**) ........... they have an accident (**5**) ........... they don't get enough food to eat. If they live, they stay with their mother for nearly two years (**6**) ........... then they must leave her to go and live alone on the ice.

There are only about 25,000 polar bears alive today. The area where you find them has many problems with pollution (**7**) ........... there are also problems with thin ice. Polar bears need your help!

**4** Read the article again and fill the spaces with **A, B** or **C.**

| | | |
|---|---|---|
| **1 A** but | **B** because | **C** or |
| **2 A** and | **B** or | **C** because |
| **3 A** or | **B** but | **C** because |
| **4 A** but | **B** because | **C** or |
| **5 A** or | **B** but | **C** because |
| **6 A** or | **B** because | **C** but |
| **7 A** because | **B** and | **C** or |

**5** Below are some sentences about Paul, a zookeeper (a person who looks after the animals in a zoo). Join the sentences together using *and, or, but* or *because*. There is sometimes more than one answer.

1 Paul looks after the elephants at a zoo. He also helps with the monkeys sometimes.
2 Paul studied in the evenings. He needed to learn about animals.
3 He takes the elephants for a walk every day. He never rides them.
4 Sometimes the elephants play with each other. Sometimes they like to lie in the sun.
5 Paul takes the elephants to the lake. The elephants like swimming there.

**SPELLING SPOT** — *their, there, they're*

*Their, there* and *they're* all sound the same but are spelled differently.

- **There** are not many polar bears in the Arctic any more.
- Polar bears spend most of **their** lives on the ice.
- When **they're** small, the polar bear cubs stay with **their** mother.

**6** Fill the spaces with *their, there* or *they're.*

I have two dogs called Wolfie and Sammy. **(1)** ................. quite small dogs. I take them for a walk in the park every day. They love it **(2)** ................. because they can play with **(3)** ................. ball and run around having fun. **(4)** ................. favourite game is chasing the ducks into the lake. **(5)** ................. always happy to go **(6)** ................. .

**7** Write a postcard to a friend about a visit to a zoo.

Say:
– where the zoo is
– who you went with
– what you did.

**Activity**

**Memory game**

- Play this game. The first person says: *I went to the zoo and I saw a lion.*
- The next person continues: *I went to the zoo and I saw a lion **and a tiger**.*
- Continue in the same way, adding another animal each time.

# Exam folder 3

## Reading Part 2   Multiple choice

Part 2 of the Reading and Writing paper tests vocabulary. There is an example and five multiple-choice questions (**6–10**). The sentences are about a topic or story. You must choose the word which best fits in the space.

Here are some examples of the types of word which are tested.
a verb – e.g. *go, made*        an adjective – e.g. *happy, nice*
a noun – e.g. *house, dog*        an adverb –  e.g. *hard, slowly*
a word which goes with another word – e.g. *have breakfast, do your homework*

| Part 2 | | | |
|---|---|---|---|
| **6** | A | B | C |
| **7** | A | B | C |
| **8** | A | B | C |
| **9** | A | B | C |
| **10** | A | B | C |

### Exam advice

- Always read the instructions and the example sentence. This will tell you what the topic is.
- Before you answer the questions, read all the sentences quickly. Together they make a short story.
- Read each sentence carefully before you decide on your answer.
- When you choose your answer, think about the meaning of the sentence.
- Read the sentence with the answer to check that the grammar is correct.
- Remember to transfer your answers to your answer sheet. There is an example of the answer sheet for Part 2 above.

## Part 2

### Questions 6–10

Read the sentences about visiting a farm.
Choose the best word (**A**, **B** or **C**) for each space.

For questions **6–10**, mark **A**, **B** or **C** on your answer sheet.

Example:

**0** Rebecca and Tom ........................ visiting their uncle's farm.
   **A** want        **B** enjoy        **C** agree

*Answer:*   **0**  A [ ]  B [■]  C [ ]

---

**6** They ........................ their dad to take them there on Saturday.
   **A** asked        **B** said        **C** talked

**7** They left home ........................ on Saturday morning.
   **A** well        **B** early        **C** ever

**8** They ........................ at the farm at 10 o'clock.
   **A** got        **B** came        **C** arrived

**9** Rebecca and Tom are always ........................ to help on the farm.
   **A** good        **B** happy        **C** kind

**10** The horses were hungry so Rebecca and Tom gave them some ........................ .
   **A** food        **B** water        **C** blankets

# Reading Part 5  Multiple choice cloze

Part 5 of the Reading and Writing paper tests grammar. There is a text with eight multiple-choice questions (**28–35**) and an example. Here are some examples of the type of words which are tested.

**Match the parts of speech (1–7) with the example words (a–g).**

1 conjunctions        a *few, several, many*
2 verb forms          b *where, when, why*
3 articles            c *and, but, because*
4 prepositions        d *done, making, had*
5 pronouns            e *a, the*
6 adjectives          f *in, at, on*
7 question words      g *he, hers, somebody*

| Part 5 | | | |
|---|---|---|---|
| 28 | A | B | C |
| 29 | A | B | C |
| 30 | A | B | C |
| 31 | A | B | C |
| 32 | A | B | C |
| 33 | A | B | C |
| 34 | A | B | C |
| 35 | A | B | C |

**Part 5**

**Questions 28–35**

Read the article about a girl and a dolphin.
Choose the best word (**A**, **B** or **C**) for each space.

For questions **28–35**, mark **A**, **B** or **C** on your answer sheet.

## The helpful dolphin

One summer I went to Florida in the USA **(0)** ........... holiday. I said goodbye to my family at the airport in London **(28)** ........... I flew to Miami. I stayed with my friend Maria. Her grandfather had a boat and we **(29)** ........... to go sailing. We had **(30)** ........... lovely time sailing! One morning I decided to sit on the side of the boat. Suddenly, I fell off into the sea. I didn't know how to swim **(31)** ........... well and I began to shout. Then, **(32)** ........... a minute I felt **(33)** ........... push me nearer the boat. **(34)** ........... was a dolphin and he was trying to help me! Maria heard me shout and her grandfather pulled me back on the boat. I **(35)** ........... now learnt to swim and I will always love dolphins!

**Example:**

**0 A** on        **B** at        **C** in        *Answer:*  | 0 | ▣ A | ☐ B | ☐ C |

28 **A** but        **B** or        **C** and
29 **A** wanted     **B** wanting   **C** want
30 **A** one        **B** a         **C** the
31 **A** very       **B** such      **C** enough
32 **A** before     **B** after     **C** since
33 **A** something  **B** anything  **C** nothing
34 **A** Him        **B** I         **C** It
35 **A** have       **B** was       **C** am

# 6.1 Theme park fun

1 Look at the photos of rides at different theme parks. Which one would you like to go on? Why? Is there a theme park near where you live? What is it called?

2 Read the information below about two theme parks called Fantasma and Alien Adventure. Decide which one you'd like to go to.

## Fantasma

☆ First opened in 1972
☆ 15 different rides
☆ Opening dates: 5th April – 2nd December
☆ Opening hours: 9.30 am – 10.30 pm
☆ 2.7 million visitors a year
☆ Hotel: 175 rooms
☆ Price: Family ticket 98 euros

## ALIEN ADVENTURE

🐜 First opened in 1950
🐜 35 different rides
🐜 Opening dates:
    1st March – 30th November
🐜 Opening hours:
    10.00 am – 10.00 pm
🐜 10.8 million visitors a year
🐜 Hotel: 990 rooms
🐜 Price: Family ticket 150 euros

3 In Part 2 of the Speaking test in KET you will need to ask and answer questions. Cover exercise 2 and ask and answer questions about Fantasma and Alien Adventure. Student A asks Student B questions about Fantasma. Student B asks Student A about Alien Adventure.

EXAMPLE: When / open?
Student A: *When did Fantasma first open?*
Student B: *It first opened in 1972.*

1 How many rides?
2 Which dates / open?
3 What / opening hours?
4 How many visitors?
5 How many hotel rooms?
6 How much / cost?

4 Look at both Fantasma and Alien Adventure and circle the correct information.

1 Fantasma is *older / newer* than Alien Adventure.
2 At Alien Adventure the opening hours are *longer / shorter* than at Fantasma.
3 Fantasma has a *bigger / smaller* hotel than Alien Adventure.
4 Alien Adventure is *more / less* expensive than Fantasma.
5 Alien Adventure has *more / fewer* visitors than Fantasma.
6 I think Alien Adventure is a *better / worse* theme park than Fantasma because it has more rides.

# Grammar

## Comparative adjectives

5  Look at the examples of comparative adjectives in exercise 4 and complete the information below.

- Short adjectives usually end in -er, e.g. (1) ...................... , (2) ...................... .
- Long adjectives usually have *more* or *less* in front of them, e.g. (3) .......................... .
- Some adjectives change completely in the comparative form, e.g. *good* and *bad* become (4) ...................... and (5) ...................... .
- Comparative adjectives are often followed by the word (6) ...................... .
- We can use (7) ...................... and *fewer* or *less* with nouns; we use (8) ...................... with countable nouns and *less* with uncountable nouns.
- See the Spelling spot for the spelling rules.

G ···〉 page 138

# Reading

6  Read the information below about theme parks.

The **biggest** and the **best!**

The first amusement park in the world was Bakken in Denmark. It opened in 1583! It had simple rides and also dancing and fireworks.

Tokyo Disneyland is <u>the most popular</u> theme park in the world. Around 17 million people visit it every year.

<u>The biggest</u> theme park is Disney World in Florida, USA.

The Drop Zone in Kings Island theme park, Ohio, USA, drops riders 80 metres from a 96-metre tower – that is the same as 9 buses on top of each other! The Drop Zone can carry up to 40 riders at a time and its top speed is 105 km per hour. It's taller than any other ride in the world.

Fujikyu Highland amusement park in Japan has a rollercoaster that travels at 170 km per hour. It is faster than any other rollercoaster. People who went on it said that it felt like being in a rocket!

# Grammar

## Superlative adjectives

Look at the words underlined in the text about theme parks. These are superlative adjectives.

- We form a superlative by adding -*est* to the end of short words and putting *the* before it.

  <u>The biggest</u> theme park is Disney World in Florida, USA.

- Longer adjectives have *the most* or *the least* in front of them.

  Tokyo Disneyland is <u>the most popular</u> theme park in the world.

7  Complete these sentences.

1  Denmark has ...................................... in the world.
2  The Drop Zone is ...................................... in the world.
3  Fujikyu Highland has ...................................... in the world.

G ···〉 page 138

---

### SPELLING SPOT

**Comparative and superlative adjectives**

- Words ending in -*y* become -*ier* in the comparative and -*iest* in the superlative.
  *easy   easier   the easiest*
- Short words ending in a vowel + consonant double the last letter.
  *hot   hotter   the hottest*

8  Complete this chart.

| adjective | comparative | superlative |
|-----------|-------------|-------------|
| boring | | |
| fast | | |
| beautiful | | |
| expensive | | |
| thin | | |
| popular | | |
| big | | |
| happy | | |

---

# 6.2 Free time

1 How often do you go shopping?
When do you listen to CDs?
What computer games do you play?
When do you see your friends?
Look at the pictures and talk about what other things you do in your free time.

## Listening

2 You will hear a girl asking for information about Aqua Park, a theme park where you can go swimming. Before you listen, read through the questions carefully and, with a partner, talk about what kind of words you think the answers will be.

EXAMPLE: *I think the answer to question 1 will be a time.*

🎧 Listen and complete the notes.

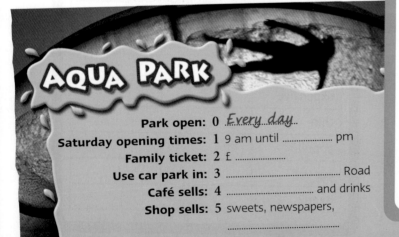

**AQUA PARK**

| | | |
|---|---|---|
| Park open: | 0 | *Every day* |
| Saturday opening times: | 1 | 9 am until ............... pm |
| Family ticket: | 2 | £ ............... |
| Use car park in: | 3 | ............... Road |
| Café sells: | 4 | ............... and drinks |
| Shop sells: | 5 | sweets, newspapers, ............... |

---

**GRAMMAR EXTRA**

**Comparative adverbs**

- Most comparative adverbs are made with *more*.
  *You can get in **more cheaply** with a family ticket.*

- Adverbs that look the same as their adjectives, for example *fast, early, hard, long, high* and a few others, for example *late, soon* use *-er* and *-est*.
  *On Saturdays we close much **later**, at ten.*

- Irregular adverbs: *well – better  badly – worse*

3 Complete the sentences with the comparative of the adverb in brackets.

1 I reached the park ...............
(soon) than I expected.
2 Angela worked ............... (hard)
than anyone else in the class.
3 Could you talk ...............
(quietly) please? I'm on the phone.
4 Pete arrived at the party
............... (early) than I did.
5 The journey took ............... (long)
this time because of the traffic.
6 Jan did ............... (well) in his
swimming exam than Carol.
7 If you can't see, move ...............
(near) the board.
8 She read the letter again
............... (careful).

4 In Part 3 of the KET Reading and Writing paper you are tested on everyday English. Look at the telephone conversations below and put them in the right order.

*Conversation 1*
a OK. No problem. Bye.
b Oh, hi, Lisa. It's Paula here. Is Serena in?
c No, she's out shopping. Can I take a message?
d No, it's Lisa.
e Bye.
f Hi, is that Serena?
g Just tell her I rang about going swimming tomorrow.
h Hello? *1*

*Conversation 2*
a Bye.
b Good morning. I'd like to book tickets for the film tonight, please.
c Three – that's for two adults and one child.
d And your name?
e Thanks very much. Bye.
f Can you collect them by 7 o'clock?
g That's fine. How many would you like?
h It's Wilkinson, W-I-L-K-I-N-S-O-N.
i Yes, no problem. Thank you.
j Hello. Can I help you? *1*

🎧 Now listen to the recording to check your answers.

5 Read this note a candidate wrote in the KET exam. There are six spelling mistakes. Can you find them and correct them?

Dear Tom,
Last Saturday I went to Aqua Park with my freind Peter. It was a beatiful day becouse the sun was shining. The Park was very intresting and their were many things wich we could do. Next time you can come with me.
Love
Simon

## Pronunciation

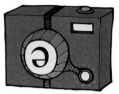

6 🎧 Listen and repeat. All the words have the /ə/ sound which is very common in English.

shorter  mother  larger
camera  banana  computer

7 Complete the crossword. All the words contain the /ə/ sound.

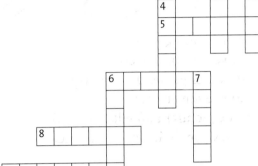

**Across**
5 The opposite of boring is …
6 You see films there.
8 Your dad.
9 Canada, the USA and Mexico.

**Down**
1 This has a keyboard.
2 Not shorter.
3 You get one in the post.
4 You do this with music.
6 You use this to take photographs.
7 By yourself.

## Activity

### Questionnaires
• In pairs, A and B, ask questions to complete the questionnaires on page 128.
• When you finish asking questions, report back to the rest of the class using comparatives and superlatives.

# Exam folder 4

## Listening Parts 4 and 5    Note taking

In Parts 4 and 5 of the Listening paper you must write down some information. In Part 4 there are always two speakers. Part 5 always has only one speaker. In both Part 4 and Part 5 there are five questions (**16–20** and **21–25**) and an example question. You must write down the word, letters or numbers that you hear.

Give the following information to your partner. Your partner should write down what you say. Spell out the words if necessary.

1  your telephone number
2  your full address
3  your favourite colour
4  your friends' first names

5  your birthday
6  a date which is important to you
7  your height
8  the cost of going to the cinema

## Exam advice

*Before listening*
- Read through the questions carefully.

*First listening*
- Don't write down the first thing you hear. Make sure you answer the question.
- Write down your answer in pencil.

*Second listening*
- Check you are correct.
- Always write something, even if you are not sure your answer is right.
- At the end of the Listening test copy your answers onto your answer sheet carefully. Check your spelling. Words that are spelled on the recording and words which are used quite often, for example, *red* or *bus*, must be spelled correctly. Below are examples of the answer sheet for Parts 4 and 5.

| Part 4 | |
| --- | --- |
| 16 | |
| 17 | |
| 18 | |
| 19 | |
| 20 | |

| Part 5 | |
| --- | --- |
| 21 | |
| 22 | |
| 23 | |
| 24 | |
| 25 | |

## Part 4

### Questions 16–20

You will hear a woman asking about a guitar for sale.
Listen and complete questions **16–20**.
You will hear the conversation twice.

---

### Guitar for Sale

| | | |
|---|---|---|
| Make of guitar: | | Fender |
| Age of guitar: | **16** | ........................ months old |
| Price: | **17** | £ |
| Address: | **18** | 60 ........................ Road |
| Bus number: | **19** | |
| Best time to visit: | **20** | after ...................... |

## Part 5

### Questions 21–25

You will hear some information about an activity centre.
Listen and complete questions **21–25**.
You will hear the information twice.

---

### High Cross Activity Centre

| | | |
|---|---|---|
| Open: | | March to October |
| Possible to do: | **21** | football, climbing, ........................ |
| Cost of one week: | **22** | £ |
| Size of largest group: | **23** | ........................ people |
| Name of manager: | **24** | Pete ........................ |
| Office telephone number: | **25** | |

# 7.1 The latest fashion

1 What is your favourite T-shirt? Talk about it, using sentences like these.

I like it because ...          On the front, it's got a picture of ...
On the back, there's a ...   I bought it in ...
The message says ...          It's the oldest / newest / most unusual T-shirt I've got.

## Reading

2 What do you know about the history of the T-shirt? Decide if these sentences are right or wrong. Don't look at the text yet.

1 In the 1940s, white T-shirts were part of a uniform.
2 T-shirts became more popular because of two 1950s American films.
3 Many women were wearing T-shirts in 1955.
4 By 1960, companies were using T-shirts to advertise their products.
5 In 1970, a T-shirt with the words 'Free Angela' won a prize.
6 Giorgio Armani included the T-shirt in his 1970s designs.
7 In 2001, one 'J'adore Dior' Christian Dior T-shirt cost almost £100.

3 Now read the text to check your answers. If there is not enough information in the text to answer right or wrong, write 'doesn't say' beside the sentence.

## THE HISTORY OF THE T-SHIRT

White cotton T-shirts were first worn by the US Navy in the Second World War and by 1948, every American soldier was wearing one too. But it was Hollywood films that made the T-shirt really popular: actors Marlon Brando and James Dean wore classic white T-shirts in *On the Waterfront* (1954) and *Rebel Without a Cause* (1955). After these films, every young man wanted to wear one.

Women didn't begin to wear T-shirts until the end of the 1950s. In the 1959 French film *A bout de souffle* (*Breathless*), American actress Jean Seberg wore a T-shirt advertising an English language newspaper. This started a new fashion in T-shirts for women, but it wasn't until the mid-1960s that companies like Budweiser and Coca-Cola started using T-shirts as 'walking advertisements'.

Later, the T-shirt became a way of saying something important. For example, soon after the black American leader Angela Davis went to prison in 1970, people all around the world were wearing T-shirts with the message 'Free Angela'.

In the 1970s, French fashion designer Yves Saint Laurent designed a famous blue T-shirt with his name in white letters. Giorgio Armani has also used T-shirts in his fashion shows. And in 2001, a limited number of white 'J'adore Dior' T-shirts sold quickly at well over £100 each!

# Grammar  Simple and continuous tenses

**4** Complete the timeline with years from the text.

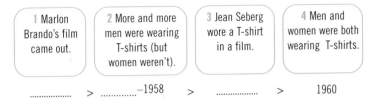

| 1 Marlon Brando's film came out. | 2 More and more men were wearing T-shirts (but women weren't). | 3 Jean Seberg wore a T-shirt in a film. | 4 Men and women were both wearing T-shirts. |

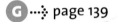

............... > ............ –1958 > ............... > 1960

**5** Which tenses are used in the underlined verbs? Why are two different tenses used in 3?

1 Hannah <u>is wearing</u> jeans today.
2 Hannah <u>wears</u> jeans nearly every day.
3 Luckily, Hannah <u>was wearing</u> jeans when she <u>fell</u> off her bike.

(G) ⋯⋗ page 139

**6** You saw a friend in a clothes shop yesterday. What was your friend doing? Make affirmative and negative sentences using these verbs.

EXAMPLE: *He was looking at some jeans.*
*He wasn't wearing a coat.*

buy   choose   look at   pay for   put on   try on   wear

**7** Put the verbs in this timeline in the correct past tense. Then complete the story.

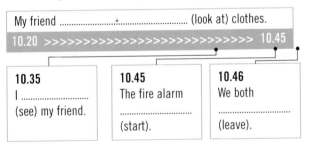

| My friend ............•............... (look at) clothes. |
|---|
| 10.20 >>>>>>>>>>>>>>>>>>>>>>>>>>> 10.45 |

| 10.35 | 10.45 | 10.46 |
|---|---|---|
| I ..................... (see) my friend. | The fire alarm ..................... (start). | We both ..................... (leave). |

Yesterday morning I (1) ...*was walking*...... (walk) around town when I (2) ..................... (see) my friend through a clothes shop window. He (3) ..................... (try on) a leather jacket, so I (4) ..................... (decide) to go inside the shop. I (5) ..................... (say) 'Hi' to my friend and then I (6) ..................... (go) to look at some jeans. I (7) ..................... (find) some really nice ones and I (8) ..................... (wait) to pay for them when the fire alarm (9) ..................... (start). We both (10) ..................... (leave) the shop immediately.

**8** Complete each sentence using the correct past tense.

1 They ......*were selling*...... (sell) beautiful T-shirts in the market last week.
2 I ..................... (buy) a really nice pair of boots in that shop.
3 Kelly ..................... (wear) a long red dress – it ..................... (look) really nice.
4 Yesterday morning I ..................... (wear) shorts, but when the sun ..................... (stop) shining I ..................... (change) into some jeans.
5 I ..................... (wait) for the bus when Jack ..................... (drive) past and ..................... (give) me a lift.
6 Tino ..................... (live) in Perugia when I last ..................... (hear) from him.

---

**SPELLING SPOT**     *-ing* form

- Verbs ending in *-e* lose this letter:
  drive → driv**ing**
  *I was **driving** beside the river when I saw a bear.*

  hope → hop**ing**
  *Mike was **hoping** to meet you last weekend.*

- Verbs ending in consonant + vowel + consonant usually double the last letter:
  begin → beginn**ing**
  *Women were **beginning** to wear shorter skirts in 1963.*

- Verbs ending in *-y* or *-w* do not double the last letter:
  pay → pay**ing**
  *I was **paying** for the jeans when I heard the alarm*

**9** Write the *-ing* forms of these verbs.

| break | make | stay | sit |
|---|---|---|---|
| leave | throw | lend | win |

# 7.2 Your clothes

1  What are your favourite clothes?
Where do you usually buy your clothes?

## Vocabulary

2  Name the clothes in the pictures.

3  Picture 1 shows *a pair of boots*. Picture 2
shows *a couple of hats*. What is the difference
between these phrases? Which other pictures
show a *pair* of something?

4  Choose a picture and use some of the words
below to describe it, but don't say the clothes
word. Guess what your partner is describing.

EXAMPLE:  *This pair has got two pockets.*
*The material looks quite light.*
(trousers – picture 16)

| adjectives | nouns |
|---|---|
| short/long | pair |
| old/new | size |
| large/small | pocket |
| dirty/clean | button |
| cheap/expensive | zip |
| heavy/light | material |
| fashionable/unfashionable | |
| leather/cotton/wool | |

## Listening

5  🎧 Listen to some English teenagers talking
about the last clothes they bought. Who
bought what? Tick the table.

|  | 1 Ben | 2 Louisa | 3 Chris |
|---|---|---|---|
| cap | | | |
| jacket | | | |
| jeans | | | |
| shirt | | | |
| shorts | | | |
| T-shirt | | | |
| trousers | | | |

## Pronunciation

**6** 🎧 Listen again to Ben and fill the spaces with the missing words. Then repeat the sentences and phrases.

**1** I ........................ as a ........................ on ........................ evenings

**2** ........................ I saw this pair of ........................ cotton shorts

**3** with lots of pockets and ........................

**4** they looked ........................

**5** with a couple of ........................ T-shirts

**7** 🎧 Now write down the words you hear. They begin with *w-*, *y-*, *z-* or *ex-*. The number of letters is given.

**1** _ _ _

**2** _ _ _ _

**3** _ _ _ _ _

**4** _ _ _ _ _ _ _ _

**5** _ _ _ _

**6** _ _ _ _ _

**7** _ _ _ _

**8** _ _ _ _ _ _ _ _

# Reading

**8** Choose A, B or C to complete these conversations.

**1** Do you have this dress in a smaller size?
   **A** You can tell.
   **B** Let me check.
   **C** No, it doesn't.

**2** You're wearing your T-shirt back to front!
   **A** Take it back then.
   **B** Yours is the best.
   **C** I prefer it like that.

**3** Is it OK to wear jeans to Sam's party?
   **A** I'm not certain.
   **B** Are you sure?
   **C** He's OK, I think.

**4** Good evening, can I take your coat?
   **A** It's mine.
   **B** Is this it?
   **C** Thank you.

**5** Bring a warm sweater for later.
   **A** Is it always warm?
   **B** Do I really need one?
   **C** How much are they?

## Activity

### Pass the hat

- For this game you need a dice and a hat per team of six.
- Give each person in the team a number from 1 to 6.
- Take turns to throw the dice. If your number is thrown, you must put on the hat and spell a clothes word.
- You get a point for every word you can spell correctly.
- You lose the hat after you have spelled three words correctly or if you spell a word wrongly. Then the dice is thrown again.
- The winner is the person with the most points.

# Writing folder 2

## Writing Part 7 Open cloze

In Part 7 of the Reading and Writing paper there is one text or two shorter texts with ten spaces (**41–50**). You must fill each space with one word. There is an example at the beginning. The text is usually a letter or a postcard.

1 Here are some examples of the kinds of words that are tested in Part 7. Can you add other words to each set?

| | |
|---|---|
| articles | *a* |
| pronouns | *it* |
| prepositions | *at* |
| quantifiers | *some* |
| auxiliary verbs | *did* |
| modal verbs | *can* |

2 Decide what kind of word should go in each space below, choosing from the list in exercise 1. Look at the words before and after the space to help you.

1 Are ......... well? *pronoun*
2 How ......... you know?
3 I went ......... the cinema.
4 You ......... eat more fruit.
5 Have you got ......... stamps?
6 What ......... pity!

3 Read these postcards and circle the correct words.

Hi Janusz!

We're having a lovely weekend (1) in / at Germany. We're staying near the centre of Berlin and there are (2) any / some great clubs near the hotel. Last night, we were dancing (3) for / until 3 am! You really (4) must / can visit this amazing city soon. Give (5) your / our love to everyone.

Enrico and Paola

Dear Enrico and Paola

Thanks for the postcard you sent me (6) from / by Berlin. It sounds fantastic. How (7) much / many was your hotel? (8) Will / Did you think it was good? Please email me their website address (9) so / because I'd like to find out more about (10) a / the hotel.

Love Janusz

## Exam advice

- Read the text quickly for general meaning.
- Work through the text sentence by sentence.
- Decide what kind of word goes in each space (look at the words before and after).
- Write your answer on the question paper first.
- Read the text again with your answers to check it makes sense.
- Check your spelling of the ten words.
- Write your answers on the answer sheet. Opposite is an example of the answer sheet for Part 7.

| Part 7 | | Do not write here |
|--------|--|-------------------|
| 41 | | 1 41 2 |
| 42 | | 1 42 2 |
| 43 | | 1 43 2 |
| 44 | | 1 44 2 |
| 45 | | 1 45 2 |
| 46 | | 1 46 2 |
| 47 | | 1 47 2 |
| 48 | | 1 48 2 |
| 49 | | 1 49 2 |
| 50 | | 1 50 2 |

## Part 7

**Questions 41–50**

Complete this letter.
Write ONE word for each space.

For questions **41–50**, write the words on your answer sheet.

**Example:** | **0** | to |

Dear Maria,

I went (**0**) .................. the town centre yesterday and I bought (**41**) .................. new clothes. Let (**42**) .................. tell you what I found. (**43**) .................. was a sale in one shop and I got two pairs of jeans (**44**) .................. the price of one! Then I decided to look in the market (**45**) .................. they sell clothes and other things very cheaply. I saw a beautiful leather belt and (**46**) .................. was only 10 euros.

You know I like T-shirts very (**47**) .................. . Well, I found a great one yesterday. The picture (**48**) .................. the front is the Mona Lisa, but the colours (**49**) .................. orange and green! This is now (**50**) .................. favourite T-shirt.

What clothes have you bought?

Love,

*Giulia*

# 8.1 A great movie

1 Can you name these films? Why are they popular? Choose from these phrases and add your own ideas.

great special effects    famous actors
wonderful story    good music

2 Ask and answer these questions.

1 What's your favourite film?
2 Who are the main actors?
3 How long is the film?
4 What's the music like?
5 Which scene in the film do you like most?

## Grammar Modal verbs 1

3 Underline the modal verbs in these sentences.

1 I can understand most films in French.
2 Jenny may buy that DVD, but she's not sure.
3 You must book in advance for the new Tom Cruise film.
4 I had to take my passport to the cinema to show my age.
5 When he was in New York, Roberto could choose to see a different movie every night.

**4** Match a–e below with sentences 1–5 in exercise 3.

   **a** talking about obligation in the present  *3*
   **b** talking about obligation in the past
   **c** talking about possibility
   **d** talking about ability in the present
   **e** talking about ability in the past

**5** Complete the grammar notes and examples.

- We cannot use the word *must* in the past. Instead, we use .h.a.d .to

   EXAMPLE: *Last night, I* ..............................
   ................................................................

- When we are talking about something we are unable to do, we use the word .................. or the contracted form ................ .

   EXAMPLE: *I* ..................................... ,
         *but I'd like to be able to.*

- If we are talking about something we were unable to do in the past, we use .................. or the contracted form ................ .

   EXAMPLE: *Before I was five, I* .................................
   ............................ , *but now I can.*

**G** ⋯⟶ page 139

**6** Circle the correct word.

   **1** Elio's just phoned. He *(can't) / couldn't* come to the cinema with us tonight.
   **2** We *must / had to* sit at the side of the cinema last time because we booked so late.
   **3** We *couldn't / can't* see very well and the seats weren't very comfortable.
   **4** There was nothing we *must / could* do about it, but this time let's book earlier!
   **5** *May / Can* you buy the tickets at lunch time?
   **6** We *may / must* all meet at the cinema no later than 7.15.
   **7** There *can / may* be time to have an ice cream after the film.
   **8** Perhaps, but I *could / must* catch the 10 o'clock bus because that's the last one.

**7** Tick the table so that it is true for you. Then compare your information with other students, using *can, can't* and *may*.

| | can | may | can't |
|---|---|---|---|
| swim 50 metres | | | |
| drive a car | | | |
| speak Chinese | | | |
| use a computer | | | |
| ski black runs | | | |
| ride a horse | | | |
| play chess | | | |
| make pizza | | | |

# Reading

**8** Read the text about Carrie-Anne Moss. Choose the best word (A, B or C) for each space.

Carrie-Anne Moss was lucky to get the part of Trinity in **THE MATRIX**. She wasn't famous at (1) ................. time, but directors Larry and Andy Wachowski knew she was the right actor for (2) ................. film. Carrie-Anne (3) ................. to do three long days of film tests to show she (4) ................. do all the difficult fight scenes. This included three hours of running and kung fu (5) ................. the first day.

In the film, the cartwheel scene (where she had to turn over and over on her hands) was the (6) ................. thing she did. During the weekend before they (7) ................. it, she was in tears, saying, 'I can't do it, I can't do it.' Then just before she did the scene, she fell badly on her foot. It hurt very (8) ................. but she kept her boots on and finished the work. Afterwards, she couldn't walk for days.

Carrie-Anne is really pleased with her work on all three **MATRIX** films – and her fans are too!

   **1 A** a     **B** (the)     **C** one
   **2 A** his    **B** its      **C** their
   **3 A** must  **B** had     **C** did
   **4 A** could  **B** can     **C** may
   **5 A** to     **B** by      **C** on
   **6 A** hard   **B** harder  **C** hardest
   **7 A** filmed  **B** filming  **C** film
   **8 A** lot    **B** much    **C** many

# 8.2 Cool sounds

1 What kinds of music do you like? Write the names of your top five bands. Which is the most popular band in your class?

## Vocabulary

2 Find ten words to do with live music in the word square (look → and ↓). The first one has been done for you. Use some of these words to talk about the band in the photo. Describe what you can see and say what each person in the band is doing.

| s | l | q | u | b | s | p | l | a | y |
|---|---|---|---|---|---|---|---|---|---|
| i | d | w | t | a | t | i | t | e | t |
| n | d | w | a | t | d | a | n | c | e |
| g | u | i | t | a | r | n | j | o | x |
| e | l | n | g | o | u | o | w | n | e |
| r | i | t | f | k | m | v | s | c | i |
| p | g | b | a | s | s | a | u | e | c |
| b | h | e | a | n | s | m | r | r | e |
| o | t | a | m | p | d | a | t | t | i |
| l | s | p | e | a | k | e | r | s | d |

## Listening

3 🎧 You will hear five short conversations. For questions 1–5, put a tick under the right answer.

1 How much did Craig earn from the concert?

£30    £45    £90

A ☐        B ☐        C ☐

2 Which band did the girl see?

A ☐        B ☐        C ☐

3 Where is the next band from?

Australia        Brazil        Iceland

A ☐        B ☐        C ☐

4 What does Ben play?

A ☐        B ☐        C ☐

5 What must Kim bring to the party?

A ☐        B ☐        C ☐

## Pronunciation

4 🎧 Listen to Anna. How does she say the short questions below?

**Boy:** *Ray's ill.*
**Anna:** *Is he?*

**Boy:** *Perhaps you can play in our band one day then.*
**Anna:** *Can I?*

🎧 Now listen to sentences 1–6. Choose the right short question from the list below. Write the sentence number next to the question. There are some questions which you will not need to use. Then listen to check your answers.

EXAMPLE: You hear: **1** *You left these CDs at the party.*

Can't you?
Did they?
Must I?
Have you?
Don't you?
Isn't it?
Aren't they?
Did I? *1*
Couldn't she?

5 🎧 Now listen again and choose a short phrase from the box to follow your question. Say the question and phrase aloud. More than one phrase may be possible.

EXAMPLE: You hear: **1** *You left these CDs at the party.*
You say: *Did I? Thanks.*

> Never mind.
> That's bad.
> What a pity.
> Thanks.
> Great news!
> How wonderful!

6 Write conversations for the three questions you didn't use in exercise 4. Include one of the short phrases from exercise 5 after each question.

### SPELLING SP T — Mistakes with vowels

Some English words contain two or three vowels together and many of these are mis-spelled by KET candidates. Look carefully at the vowels used in these words.

| beautiful | idea | easy | museum |
|-----------|------|------|--------|
| favourite | because | friend | tourist |

7 Here are some errors that candidates have made in the KET exam. Correct the sentences.

1 Yesterday I was at a beatiful rock concert.
2 It's my favrit cinema.
3 I'm selling my piano becouse I don't want it any more.
4 A lot of turists visit my town.
5 I went to a nightclub with my freends.
6 There are two musuems in the town.

### Activity

#### Who is it?

- Look at the photo. Can you guess who's under the hat and sunglasses? Read the sentences below the picture to help you decide.

*This person sings rap music and has a band. In 2002, he earned around $29 million. He was in the film 'Eight Mile'.*

- Make a poster for the classroom wall about a musician of your choice. Find a picture of him or her but make it difficult to see who it is. Include some sentences about your person below the picture.

## Speaking

1 Read these sentences with a partner. Say what you think about each one and give some extra information.

1 It's bad to keep animals in zoos.
2 Ten years ago, people in offices couldn't wear jeans.
3 The best thing about today's films is the special effects.
4 We must all look after the planet.
5 Students can get into museums and theme parks more cheaply than adults.

## Grammar

2 In **1–4** only one sentence (**A–C**) is correct. Tick the correct sentence.

1 A I bought a green trousers yesterday.
  B I bought some green trouser yesterday.
  C I bought a pair of green trousers yesterday.

2 A We could to wait half an hour to go on our favourite ride.
  B We had to wait half an hour to go on our favourite ride.
  C We must to wait half an hour to go on our favourite ride.

3 A Enzo was playing drums when he was dropping his drumstick.
  B Enzo played drums when he dropped his drumstick.
  C Enzo was playing drums when he dropped his drumstick.

4 A The band's new singer sings very well.
  B The band's new singer sings very best.
  C The band's new singer sings very good.

3 Read the text about a famous film. Choose the best word (**A, B** or **C**) for each space.

| | | | |
|---|---|---|---|
| 1 | A by | B with | C from |
| 2 | A good | B better | C best |
| 3 | A but | B when | C if |
| 4 | A on | B into | C at |
| 5 | A takes | B taken | C took |
| 6 | A so | B and | C because |
| 7 | A much | B lots | C many |
| 8 | A also | B too | C both |

(1 B with — circled)

The film 'Pirates of the Caribbean' had a wonderful story, (1) ............ really great special effects. The (2) ............ actor in the film was Johnny Depp, who played the pirate Jack Sparrow. Jack was a clever sailor (3) ............ he lost his ship, the Black Pearl, to a very bad pirate called Captain Barbossa.

Barbossa sailed (4) ............ the town of Port Royal and (5) ............ a beautiful young girl called Elizabeth away as his prisoner. Jack Sparrow agreed to help find Elizabeth (6) ............ he wanted to get his ship back.

Of course, there is (7) ............ of adventure in this film. It is (8) ............ very funny.

# Vocabulary

4 Complete each sentence with an adjective from the box. Use each adjective once only.

boring closed fast hot
old small ~~tall~~ thin

1 Henry was so ....._tall_..... that he couldn't stand up straight in the room.
2 I'm going to change into a T-shirt – it's too ..................... to wear a sweater.
3 We tried to go on one more ride, but it was ..................... .
4 This book is so ..................... – nothing interesting ever happens!
5 I've had these ..................... football boots for too long.
6 Eurostar trains go really ..................... so you can get to places quickly.
7 Because they diet a lot, most fashion models are very ..................... .
8 Most dogs are not as ..................... as cats.

5 Put these words into four meaning groups.

~~bear~~ ~~blouse~~ button chess climbing concert cycling dolphin drums elephant fish guitar horse jacket monkey piano pocket shorts skateboarding snake socks song table tennis trainers zip

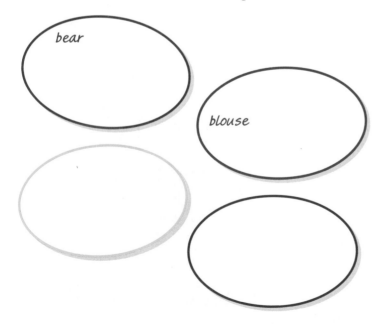

bear

blouse

# Writing

6 Complete this letter about visiting a theme park in France. Write ONE word for each space.

Hi Steffi,

My parents took us (1) ............. Parc Astérix, just north of Paris, yesterday. (2) ............. was fantastic! In the morning, we (3) ............. driving up the A1 motorway from Paris when my younger brother saw a big sign with Astérix on. He laughed and screamed – he was (4) ............. excited than I was!

We spent eight hours (5) ............. the park and enjoyed everything – the rides, the little plays outside and the wild boar sandwiches! The (6) ............. thing for me was meeting Obélix (7) ..................... he is my favourite person in the stories. My brother asked him about (8) ............. red hair and we got a photo of us all together.

We (9) ............. go there again (my dad isn't sure). If we do, (10) ............. don't you come too?

Love,

Amélie

# 9.1 Making holiday plans

**1** What's your idea of the perfect holiday? Tell your partner.

## Listening

**2** 🎧 Listen to four people talking about their plans for their next holiday. Match the people to the places and the type of holiday. The first one has been done for you.

| 1 Julie | Greece | sailing |
| 2 Daniel | France | walking |
| 3 Simon | Australia | camping |
| 4 Natalie | Switzerland | beach |

🎧 Then listen again and write down how they are going to travel.

**5** Julie – by ..............................
**6** Daniel – by ..............................
**7** Simon – by ..............................
**8** Natalie – by ..............................

## Grammar   The future with *going to*

- When we intend to do something in the future, we use *to be going to*.
  **I'm going to** do some walking in Switzerland.

  I decided to do it        I'm going to do it
  *past*                    *now*                    *future*

- With the verb *to go* we often don't repeat the *to go* and just say, for example, *I'm going to the travel agent's tomorrow.*

**G** ⋯▸ page 140

**3** Look at the pictures below. Take turns to ask and answer questions.

EXAMPLE:
A: *Look at picture 1.*
   *What's she going to do?*
B: *She's going to catch a plane.*

**4** Complete these sentences using *to be going to* + one of the verbs from the box.

close ~~stay~~ do have meet book telephone visit

1 I had a terrible holiday last year. Next year
  ...........*I'm going to stay*.......... at home.
2 Peter ........................................ the hotel
  and ask for a room with a view.
3 After lunch Sue and Liz ........................................
  ........................ some shopping for souvenirs.
4 I ........................................ my flight
  early next time. It may be cheaper.
5 The cruise ship ........................................
  Athens, Naples and Nice.
6 The management ........................................
  the pool today because it needs cleaning.
7 We ........................................ our
  friends later, in the café.
8 We ........................................ a camping
  holiday again next year.

## Pronunciation /h/

**5** Look at the words below.
Underline the words
which contain the
sound /h/.

hand  holiday  why  home  hill  when
honest  how  happy  hour  school  hotel

🎧 Listen to check your answers.

**6** Put the words in each sentence into the right order.

1 home hills has a he holiday in the
2 a hopes birthday Helen get horse for her she'll
3 homework him with his help
4 have holiday happy a
5 hire boat fun and have going I'm to a
6 helicopter me into the help

🎧 Listen to check your answers.

**7** 🎧 Listen and circle the word you hear.

1 eye / (high)    4 and / hand    6 all / hall
2 old / hold     5 air / hair     7 art / heart
3 it / hit

# Reading

**8** In KET Reading paper Part 3 you must complete a conversation.

Complete the conversation. What does Stella say to the travel agent? Choose from replies A–H below. There are two extra replies that you don't need to use.

EXAMPLE:
**Travel agent:** Good morning. Can I help you?
**Stella:**      0 ......*H*......

**Travel agent:** Where would you like to go?
**Stella:**      1 ................
**Travel agent:** Florida is very popular.
**Stella:**      2 ................
**Travel agent:** It is all year, but there are lots of hotels.
**Stella:**      3 ................
**Travel agent:** Well, what about a holiday centre in Sardinia?
**Stella:**      4 ................
**Travel agent:** Yes, you can fly there easily and this year the price is only going to be 450 euros a week.
**Stella:**      5 ................
**Travel agent:** That's fine. Take some of these brochures so you can both look at them at home.

A Isn't it very busy in summer?
B Oh, that's more than I thought! I'm going to have to talk to my friend first.
C I'm not sure. I like places where I can do lots of things.
D Really? I thought the beach was good.
E That sounds more interesting. Is it easy to get to?
F No, I have a couple of weeks free.
G I'm not sure. What else do you have?
H Yes, please. I'd like to book a holiday.

An American, called Dennis Tito, paid $20 million for a trip in a Russian spacecraft in 2001.

The travel company Thomas Cook has 6,000 people waiting for a place on its *Lunar Tours*.

1 Say if these reasons will or won't make people want to holiday on the moon or in space.

EXAMPLE:

the views of Earth – *I think the views of Earth will be so good that people will want to go into space to see them.*

the views of Earth     the weather
the journey            the activities/attractions
the scenery            the accommodation
the food               the price

## Reading

The World Tourism Organisation says that space will soon be a popular place to go on holiday – possibly by 2020. One Japanese company is getting ready. They are planning a space holiday centre. It will look like a bicycle wheel and have a hotel for 100 people and a theme park. It will travel round the Earth at a height of 300 km. The company hopes the centre will be ready in 2017. The company chairman says he thinks that flying to the centre will probably be quicker than flying from Hong Kong to Singapore. When they are on board the centre, tourists will take short trips to the moon or go for walks in space. But what about the cost? Well, the company believes that people will be happy to pay about $100,000 for a trip but they think that as more people want to go, the trip will become much cheaper.

An American hotel group is also thinking of building a hotel, called the Lunar Hotel. This will be on the moon. Most of the hotel will be under the ground so it won't become too hot or too cold. The rooms will look just like they do on Earth with curtains, carpets, plants and they will have wall-to-wall television. The guests will eat normal food for lunch. The cooks will just push a button to mix dried food with water to become an instant meal! There will be little or no dirt and there won't be much water, so the hotel won't wash the towels and sheets – it will throw them away!

2 Read the article about holidays in space and then write questions for the answers 1–7.

1 A bicycle wheel.
   *What will the holiday centre look like?*
2 100
3 300 km
4 2017
5 Go for walks in space.
6 $100,000
7 Under the ground.

## Grammar  The future with *will*

- We use *will / 'll* + verb or *will not / won't* + verb to talk about the future.
  *Space **will** soon be a popular place to go on holiday.*
  *The hotel **won't** wash the towels and sheets.*

- We often use these words with the future simple:
  *probably    certainly    definitely    possibly*

- When we are predicting something we also often use *think + will*.
  *The company chairman says he **thinks** that flying to the centre **will** probably be quicker than flying from Hong Kong to Singapore.*

**3** What will happen in the future? Write some sentences about each topic below. Use *will* or *won't*. When you have finished, tell your partner what your ideas are.

EXAMPLE: travel
*I think that travel by plane will probably become cheaper.*
*I think beach holidays will certainly be less popular.*

1 travel
2 yourself
3 your best friend
4 your favourite football team
5 your favourite band
6 your school

**G** ···⟩ page 140

---

**SPELLING SPOT**  ⬭ Words ending in *-y*

- Usually when we add an ending to words ending in *-y*, the *-y* changes to *-i*.
  *baby – babies, hurry – hurried,*
  *funny – funnier, carry – carries*
- But *-y* does not change to *-i* if the word ends in *-ay, -ey, -oy* or *-uy*.
  *boy – boys, stay – stayed*

**4** Complete each sentence with a word from the box in the correct form.

| buy | enjoy | family | happy | ~~holiday~~ |
|-----|-------|--------|-------|---------|
| key | monkey | play | stay | study |

1 We had many happy __holidays__ in Chile.
2 Shakespeare's ............................. are known all over the world.
3 Lucy is much ............................. now she has a new flat.
4 I've lost my ............................. and can't get into the house.
5 We like the ............................. best at the zoo.
6 Ben is ............................. Italian at university.
7 Dr Turner very much ............................. the film he saw last night.
8 Sheila always ............................. at the same hotel when she's in Rome.
9 I think big ............................. are much more fun than small ones.
10 She ............................. her clothes from a well-known designer.

---

**5** Read this email from Susie, who is on holiday on the moon. Decide which word (1–10) below) best fits each space.

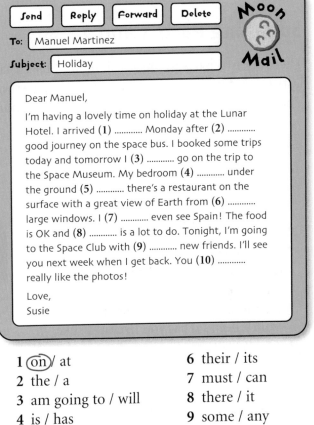

| Send | Reply | Forward | Delete |

**To:** Manuel Martinez
**Subject:** Holiday

Dear Manuel,

I'm having a lovely time on holiday at the Lunar Hotel. I arrived (**1**) ............ Monday after (**2**) ............ good journey on the space bus. I booked some trips today and tomorrow I (**3**) ............ go on the trip to the Space Museum. My bedroom (**4**) ............ under the ground (**5**) ............ there's a restaurant on the surface with a great view of Earth from (**6**) ............ large windows. I (**7**) ............ even see Spain! The food is OK and (**8**) ............ is a lot to do. Tonight, I'm going to the Space Club with (**9**) ............ new friends. I'll see you next week when I get back. You (**10**) ............ really like the photos!

Love,
Susie

1 (on)/ at               6 their / its
2 the / a                7 must / can
3 am going to / will     8 there / it
4 is / has               9 some / any
5 or / but               10 will / do

---

**Activity**

**Are you a World Traveller?**

- Read the questionnaire on page 129 and ask and answer the questions with a partner.
- Look at the scores on page 130 to find out if your partner is a

  *World Traveller*
  *Happy Tourist*
  *Stay-at-Home.*

# Exam folder 5

## Speaking Parts 1 and 2

There are two parts to the Speaking test. Part 1 lasts for 5–6 minutes and Part 2 lasts for 3–4 minutes. You do the Speaking test with another student.
There are two examiners – one who asks questions and one who listens.

### Exam advice

- If you don't understand, ask the examiner: *Could you repeat the question, please?*
- Speak clearly.
- Don't worry if the other student knows more or less English than you do. It's what you say that is important.
- Practise giving information about yourself and what you like or dislike.
- Check you can describe places and subjects so you can answer questions about why you like something.
- Always say something, even if you are not sure you are right.
- Practise asking and answering questions.

### Part 1

In Part 1 you are asked questions about yourself, your hobbies, your studies, etc. You will hear some examples of the type of questions on the recording.

1 🎧 Listen to a student talking to an examiner. The first time, listen to get a general idea of what happens in Part 1.

🎧 Then listen again and complete this chart.

| Name: | |
|---|---|
| Town/country: | |
| Favourite subject(s): | |
| Free time activity: | |
| Countries visited: | |

2 Ask and answer these questions.

EXAMPLE:
What / name? *What's your name?*

How spell / surname?
Where / come from?
Where / study?
What subjects / study?
Which subject / like best?
Where / go on holiday?
What / do next weekend?
Have / been to other countries?

## Part 2

In Part 2 you will need to ask and answer questions. The examiner will give Candidate A a card with some information on it and Candidate B a card with some questions. Then Candidate B will be given a card with some information on it and Candidate A will be given a card with some questions.

3  Candidate A, here is some information about a holiday centre.
   Candidate B, you don't know anything about the holiday centre, so ask A some questions about it. You will find the questions on page 131.

**Holiday Centre**

### Westcliffe on Sea

★ Lots of fun for all the family!

★ Open March – November

★ Swimming pool and tennis courts

★ Excellent restaurant

Cost of a week in July: Adults £400  Children £250

4  Candidate B, here is some information about a cinema. Candidate A, you don't know anything about the cinema, so ask B some questions about it. You will find the questions on page 132.

Burford Arts Cinema
68 Helman Street
Burford

**This week only**

# The Return
of the
# Martians

An adventure film starring Tom Schroder

Every day at 2.00 pm

Tickets: Adults £7.00 Children £3.50 Students £5.00

Eat at our Riverside Café – open all day and every evening.

colour key (left margin): blue, black, brown, green, grey, orange, pink, red, white, yellow, purple

## Vocabulary

1 Match the words 1–15 with the pictures a–o.

1 lamp *h*      9 DVD player
2 wardrobe      10 sofa
3 bed           11 desk
4 CD player     12 bookshelves
5 mirror        13 curtains
6 chair         14 computer
7 poster        15 light
8 floor

2 Talk about your room. What's it like? You can use some of the ideas below.

It's large.
It's got a single bed.
It's painted pink.
There's a poster on the wall.
It's on the first floor.
It's got a comfortable chair.
It's very untidy.

---

**SPELLING SPOT**   **Words ending in -f, -fe**

- Nouns ending in *-f* or *-fe* usually change to *-ves* in the plural: *half – halves*
- Some nouns *don't* change: *roof – roofs, café – cafés.*

3 Make the underlined words plural.

  1 There's a shelf in the kitchen.
    *There are some shelves in the kitchen.*
  2 I have a bookshelf in my room.
  3 The knife is on the table.
  4 The roof is red.
  5 His wife is in the kitchen.
  6 I found a leaf on the floor.

## Listening

4 Look at the objects 1–6, and the list of rooms. With a partner, decide which room or rooms the objects are usually found in.

EXAMPLE: *You usually find a desk in a teenager's bedroom.*

1 a desk          a bathroom
2 a sofa          a bedroom
3 a computer      a dining room
4 a CD player     a hall
5 a mirror        a kitchen
6 a bookshelf     a living room

**5** 🎧 Listen to a conversation between a girl called Lisa and her friend Tom about her family's new flat. She is telling him in which room (**A–H**) the family has put the objects 0–5.

For questions 1–5, write a letter A–H next to each object.

EXAMPLE:

**0** the metal desk  *E*

**1** the leather sofa  D    **A** the bathroom
**2** the computer  *F*    **B** the hall
**3** the CD player  H    **C** the living room
**4** the large mirror  A    **D** the dining room
**5** the new bookshelves  B    **E** the garage
                         **F** Lisa's bedroom
                         **G** the kitchen
                         **H** her parents' bedroom

## Vocabulary

**6** Ask and answer questions.

EXAMPLE: A: *What's the vase made of?*
             B: *It's made of glass.*

             B: *What are the curtains made of?*
             A: *They're made of cotton.*

| wood | leather | paper | metal | silver |
| --- | --- | --- | --- | --- |
| glass | gold | wool | plastic | cotton |

**7** Match each adjective with its opposite.

large            short
narrow        single
big              hard
new            old
cold           small
expensive      low
high           cheap
noisy          hot
soft            quiet
long           wide
double        little

**8** Read the sentences about a flat. Choose the best word (**A, B** or **C**) for each space.

**1** The bedroom is very .................. and there isn't enough room for a double bed.
     **A** short      **B** narrow      **C** single

**2** The flat is .................. at night because there's no traffic noise.
     **A** soft      **B** low      **C** quiet

**3** My new bed is very .................. and hurts my back.
     **A** hard      **B** long      **C** wide

**4** Our flat is very .................. up so we have a good view of the park.
     **A** high      **B** big      **C** new

**5** I have a very .................. CD player in my bedroom.
     **A** double      **B** expensive      **C** soft

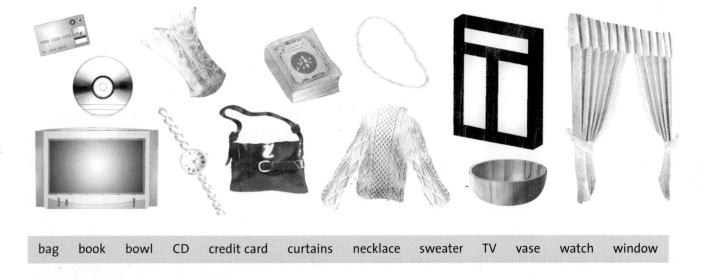

| bag | book | bowl | CD | credit card | curtains | necklace | sweater | TV | vase | watch | window |

# 10.2 Famous buildings

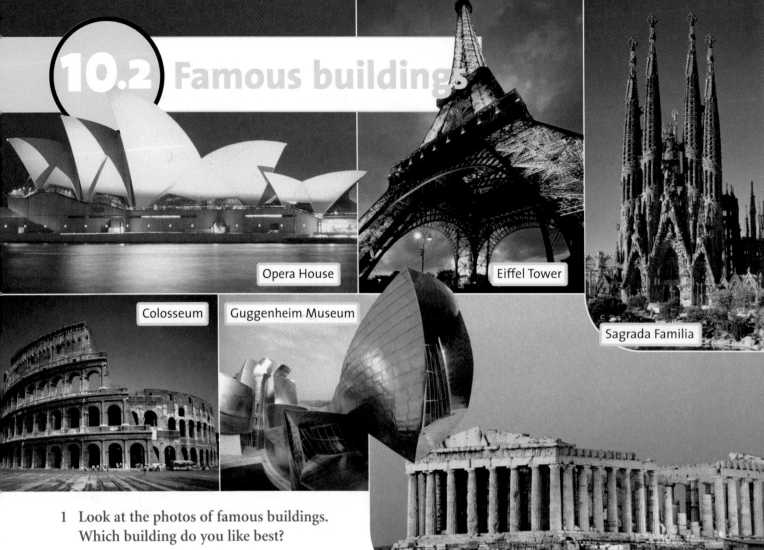

Opera House

Eiffel Tower

Colosseum

Guggenheim Museum

Sagrada Familia

Parthenon

1 Look at the photos of famous buildings. Which building do you like best?

Match each building with the correct place, date and builder.

EXAMPLE: *The Eiffel Tower was built in Paris between 1887 and 1889 by Gustav Eiffel.*

| | | |
|---|---|---|
| Rome | 1887–9 | Gustav Eiffel |
| Paris | 447–432 BC | Jørn Utzon |
| Bilbao | 1959–73 | Antonio Gaudí |
| Athens | AD 70–82 | Pericles |
| Barcelona | 1997 | Frank Gehry |
| Sydney | 1884–the present | Vespasian |

## Pronunciation

2 Write these dates as words.

EXAMPLE: *1173 – eleven seventy-three*

**1** 1292 **2** 1569 **3** 1718 **4** 1890 **5** 1963

🎧 Listen and check.

3 🎧 Listen and write down the dates you hear.

## Grammar

We can say:
   *Gustav Eiffel **built** the Eiffel Tower in Paris between 1887 and 1889.*
This sentence is **active** and Gustav Eiffel is the subject of the sentence.

Or we can say:
   *The Eiffel Tower **was built** in Paris between 1887 and 1889 by Gustav Eiffel.*
This sentence is **passive** and the Eiffel Tower is now the subject of the sentence. We use *by* to say who did the action.
This is an example of the **past simple passive**.

The passive is formed by using *to be* + the past participle of the verb.

**G** ⋯﹕ page 141

**4** Complete these sentences with the verb in brackets in the present simple passive or past simple passive.

1 When Paul arrived at the White House he (take) ........was taken........ to see the President.
2 My watch (make) ........................... by a factory in Switzerland.
3 A library is a place where books (borrow) ........................... .
4 Kim's bedroom (paint) ........................... last month.
5 Their house (sell) ........................... for £250,000.
6 The Houses of Parliament (build) ........................... more than 150 years ago.
7 Children (teach) ........................... in a school.
8 The flat (buy) ........................... for her by her father.

**5** Complete the article about the London Eye with the verbs in brackets in either the active or passive form.

**6** Complete the questions and find the answers in the article in exercise 5 below.

1 Who / design the London Eye?
  *Who designed the London Eye?*
  *It was designed by David Marks and Julia Barfield.*
2 When / competition / organise?
3 How many / carry?
4 Where / wheel / develop?
5 Where / capsules / make?
6 Who / produce / glass?

**Activity**

## What's the connection?

- Play in pairs.
- Place a pile of cards between you.
- Each person takes a card in turn and has to say what the two things on the card have in common, using either the past simple passive or the present simple passive.

  EXAMPLE: a wardrobe and a chest of drawers
  *Possible answer:*
  *They are both made of wood.*

- Only one answer is necessary and a correct answer gets a point.
- The winner is the person who gets the most points.

**The London Eye** is one of the most popular attractions in London, and it (**0**) ..*is visited*.. (visit) by people from all over the UK and the world. It (**1**) ........................... (design) by David Marks and Julia Barfield for a competition which (**2**) ........................... (organise) by a British newspaper in 1994. The newspaper (**3**) ........................... (want) a new London building to celebrate the year 2000.
  The Eye is 135 metres tall and it is the largest observation wheel in the world. Up to 800 people (**4**) ........................... (carry) on it at any one time. Marks and Barfield (**5**) ........................... (design) and (**6**) ........................... (build) the Eye in less than 16 months. More than 1,700 people (**7**) ........................... (work) on building the London Eye and much of it (**8**) ........................... (build) in other countries. The wheel (**9**) ........................... (develop) in the Netherlands. Experts in the Czech Republic and Italy (**10**) ........................... (make) some of the metal parts. The capsules which the people sit in (**11**) ........................... (make) in the French Alps and the glass (**12**) ........................... (produce) in Italy.

# Exam folder 6

## Reading Part 4  Right, Wrong, Doesn't say

In Part 4 of the Reading and Writing paper, there is a text with seven questions (**21–27**) and an example.

### Exam advice

- Read all the text carefully to get an idea of what it is about.
- For each question, find the right part of the text then read it again carefully.
- The questions are in the order in which you will find the answers in the text.
- Don't try to guess the answer or answer it from your own experience. You must find the answer in the text.
- If you can't find the information, then it is probably a *Doesn't say* question.
- Don't worry if you don't understand every word.
- Practise filling in the answer on your answer sheet. (See opposite for an example.)

| Part 4 | A | B | C |
|---|---|---|---|
| 21 | ☐ | ☐ | ☐ |
| 22 | ☐ | ☐ | ☐ |
| 23 | ☐ | ☐ | ☐ |
| 24 | ☐ | ☐ | ☐ |
| 25 | ☐ | ☐ | ☐ |
| 26 | ☐ | ☐ | ☐ |
| 27 | ☐ | ☐ | ☐ |

## Part 4

### Questions 21–27

Read the article about a visit to Hearst Castle, a famous building in California.

Are the sentences **21–27** 'Right' (**A**) or 'Wrong' (**B**)?
If there is not enough information to answer 'Right' (**A**) or 'Wrong' (**B**), choose 'Doesn't say' (**C**).

### A visit to Hearst Castle
**by Theresa Martin**

Last year, I had a great trip to Hearst Castle at San Simeon in California. Hearst Castle was built by William Randolph Hearst between 1922 and 1939, at a cost of more than $30 million – about $277 million today.

I spent all day looking around, but it wasn't enough. There was so much to see. Hearst Castle is really four houses. The main house, 'Casa Grande', is much bigger than the other three, which were used for guests. Many of these were Hollywood film stars, and they often came to Hearst's parties.

At Hearst Castle, there are 56 bedrooms, 61 bathrooms and 19 sitting rooms. There are also beautiful gardens, a garage for 25 large cars and two swimming pools, one inside and a larger one outside. I loved the one outside, the 'Neptune Pool' – it was a pity we couldn't go swimming!

I found the tour very helpful. The guide told me that Hearst, at the age of ten, toured Europe with his mother, looking at paintings and castles. He never forgot this tour and decided that he wanted his house to look like a castle.

Hearst died in 1951, and Hearst Castle was given by his family to the people of California. It is now a museum.

**Examples:**

**0**   Hearst Castle was cheap to build.

*The answer is **B** (Wrong) because the text says the castle cost 'more than $30 million' to build.*

**00**   Theresa wanted to spend more time at Hearst Castle.

*The answer is **A** (Right) because the text says that Theresa 'spent all day looking around, but it wasn't enough'.*

**000** Hearst Castle is on a mountain near the sea.

*The answer is **C** (Doesn't say) because there is no information in the text which tells you exactly where the castle is.*

---

**21** Hearst's guests stayed in 'Casa Grande'.

   **A** Right     **B** Wrong     **C** Doesn't say

**22** The swimming pools are the same size.

   **A** Right     **B** Wrong     **C** Doesn't say

**23** Theresa thought the tour was very useful.

   **A** Right     **B** Wrong     **C** Doesn't say

**24** Hearst enjoyed living at Hearst Castle.

   **A** Right     **B** Wrong     **C** Doesn't say

**25** Hearst remembered his trip to Europe all his life.

   **A** Right     **B** Wrong     **C** Doesn't say

**26** Hearst died in Hearst Castle.

   **A** Right     **B** Wrong     **C** Doesn't say

**27** The Hearst family still live at Hearst Castle.

   **A** Right     **B** Wrong     **C** Doesn't say

# 11.1 Living for sport

snowboarding

baseball

windsurfing

tennis

basketball

1 Do you play/do any of the sports in the photos? Which sports do you enjoy watching? Why?

## Vocabulary

2 Say which words go with each sport in the photos. You can use some words several times.

| | | | | |
|---|---|---|---|---|
| ball | basket | bat | board | boots |
| court | glove(s) | net | racket | sail |

3 🎧 Listen to five teenagers talking about the sports in the photos. Say what each sport is. Do they *play/do* the sport or *watch* it?

| | sport | play/do or watch? |
|---|---|---|
| Speaker 1 | | |
| Speaker 2 | | |
| Speaker 3 | | |
| Speaker 4 | | |
| Speaker 5 | | |

4 Which sport does a *striker* play? Find ten more words about the same sport in this word square (look → and ↓).

| e | s | t | r | i | k | e | r |
|---|---|---|---|---|---|---|---|
| a | c | u | p | b | h | o | e |
| n | o | t | g | o | a | l | t |
| e | r | e | f | e | r | e | e |
| t | e | c | l | u | b | k | a |
| m | a | t | c | h | a | i | m |
| o | n | l | i | r | t | c | o |
| b | o | o | t | s | e | k | t |

## Pronunciation

5 🎧 Listen and repeat.

basketball    bigger    boots    bought
vegetable    video    village    volleyball

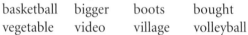

1 Bob plays basketball.
2 Brenda bought some new boots.
3 I live in a very small village.
4 There's a very good video on volleyball.
5 Bill eats bread and vegetables before he plays volleyball.

6 Write a sentence using as many words beginning with *b* and *v* as you can. It can be as funny as you like! Read your sentence to your classmates.

# Reading

7 Here is part of an interview with Michael Owen, the famous England football player. Read questions 1–5 carefully. Then decide which answer Michael gives to each question: A, B or C.

 **You started playing for Liverpool at 17. What was it like playing big matches then?**

A I'm older now, but I still enjoy playing.
B When you're that age, you don't think. It's just a game.
C Some stadiums are bigger now and they're always full.

② **When did you first play for your country?**

A I was a different player against Argentina in the World Cup.
B I remember the matches in Germany and Brazil.
C I played for the England schoolboys team.

③ **What is the most important thing about the game for you?**

A I was born near Liverpool, but many clubs haven't got any local players.
B Football is very important in my life, but I enjoy golf too.
C A striker has got to get the ball into the net. I live to score goals.

④ **You run very fast! Can you explain why?**

A It usually takes me about 35 or 40 minutes to drive home from the club.
B My dad, and my mum as well, were both quick when they were young. All their kids are flying machines!
C When I came back from the 1998 World Cup in France, I scored three goals for Liverpool at Newcastle.

⑤ **Michael, what makes a top football player extra special?**

A You have to have something in your head. You need a good body, but you need to think too.
B The fans like to see us buy a foreign player for 10 or 20 million.
C I didn't know all the players' names then. Now I know them all.

8 What do you know about Michael Owen now? Write five short sentences about him, using some of the information from the interview.

EXAMPLE: *He played in the 1998 World Cup.*

## GRAMMAR EXTRA

**Word order in questions**

**Yes/No questions**
*Can you explain?*
*Does Giulio play basketball?*

**Wh- questions**
*What happened?*
(*What* is the subject of the sentence.)
*Who scored the most baskets?*
(*Who* is the subject of the sentence.)
*What do you know about Michael Owen?*
(*What* is the object of the sentence.)

9 Put these words in the right order to make questions.

1 tennis / you / play / can
   *Can you play tennis?*
2 team / Totti / which / does / play for
3 got / a snowboard / you / have
4 the next / World Cup / is / when
5 didn't / why / go / you / to the match
6 is / favourite / which / sport / your
7 does / the referee / where / come / from
8 want to / in the competition / swim / you / do

10 Write five questions using the card below. Compare your questions with a partner. Then Student A ask the questions. Student B turn to page 131 and answer the questions.

**SPORTS COMPETITION AT THIS COLLEGE**
- when?
- sports?
- where?
- what / clothes?
- prizes?

# 11.2 Keeping fit

1 Do you do anything to keep fit or do you hate taking exercise?

2 Answer the questions in this chart and find out who you are like.

**Start here**

Do you like watching TV? ← NO — Do you take regular exercise? — YES → Do you do a lot of sport?

Do you stay inside when it rains?

Do you spend more time playing computer games than going out with your friends?

Is winning important to you?

Do you keep taking the lift not the stairs?

Do you hate walking to school?

Is relaxing sometimes better than exercising?

**TIRED TOMATO**

You are happiest in bed, on the sofa or sleeping in a maths lesson. Try to get out more. Why not do something new? Start playing some sport.

**HAPPY HEART**

You know the correct mix in life. Why not ride your bike round the town for an hour and then eat a big bar of chocolate when you get home!

**FITNESS FREAK**

Wow! Don't you ever stop exercising? It's good to do exciting things but you have to learn to relax too. Why not spend the evening in front of the TV?

## Grammar  Verbs in the -ing form

3 There are several examples of verbs in the -ing form in the chart, for example, *Do you like <u>watching</u> TV?* Find ten examples in the chart and underline them.

4 The -ing is added to the infinitive of the verb:
watch + -ing = watching
*I enjoy watching TV.*

Sometimes there is a spelling change. Write the -ing forms of these verbs. Look back at the Spelling spot on page 45 if necessary.

| | | |
|---|---|---|
| 1 sit | 4 get | 7 run |
| 2 make | 5 drive | 8 throw |
| 3 swim | 6 play | 9 carry |

5 Complete these sentences with a verb from the box in the -ing form.

> go   hit   move   play   practise
> ~~wait~~   walk   win

1 Jess really enjoys snowboarding but she hates ......*waiting*...... for the chair lifts up the mountain.
2 Please stop ........................... the ball outside the court – we'll lose it!
3 I don't mind ........................... in goal but I really want to be a striker.
4 I feel like ........................... for a run. Do you want to come?
5 Keep ........................... your arms and legs or you'll get cold.
6 If we start ........................... now, it'll take us an hour to get home.
7 Mark doesn't spend enough time ........................... his golf shots.
8 If the team keeps ........................... every week, we'll soon be at the top!

**6** Now say how you feel about the activities below, using verbs in the *-ing* form. You can add *really* to make the sentence stronger.

EXAMPLE: *I really enjoy exercising at the gym!*

☺                ☺                ☹
love          don't mind       hate
enjoy
like

1 exercise at the gym          5 swim at the pool
2 run along the beach          6 walk to school
3 climb stairs                 7 dance with my friends
4 play computer games          8 go for a bike ride

**G** ···⟫ page 141

## Listening

**7** 🎧 You will hear some information about a fitness club. Listen and complete questions 1–5.

### Solway Fitness Club

Opening hours: (**1**) 6.30 am – ............................ pm

For gym introduction, phone Jack Bergman: (**2**) 0453 ............................

Swimming pool: (**3**) ............................ metres

To become a member, speak to: (**4**) Mrs ............................

Guided tours on: (**5**) ............................ afternoon

---

**SPELLING SPOT**                                    gu-, qu-

Remember you sometimes need to include the letter *u* after *g* if it is pronounced /g/, as in *guided tour*. The letter *u* always follows *q*, as in *queen*.

**8** Spell the words that have these meanings.

1 fast (adverb)                          q _ _ _ _ _ _
2 one of four parts of something         q _ _ _ _ _ _
3 a musical instrument                   g _ _ _ _ _
4 a person staying at a hotel            g _ _ _ _
5 not saying anything (adjective)        q _ _ _ _
6 if you don't know the answer, you have to do this   g _ _ _ _

**9** Read the descriptions of some sports. What is the word for each one? The first letter is already there.

1 You can get to the bottom of a mountain quite fast by doing this.
  s _ _ _ _ _
2 You need a bike to do this sport.
  c _ _ _ _ _ _
3 This sport lets you catch something to eat!
  f _ _ _ _ _ _
4 If you do this sport, practise on easy hills first.
  c _ _ _ _ _ _ _
5 Your boat needs some wind for this sport.
  s _ _ _ _ _ _

### Activity

**Find out who ...**

- Organise a class survey to find out who ...
  - ▸ takes the most exercise each week
  - ▸ plays the largest number of different sports
  - ▸ watches the most football matches
  - ▸ knows about an unusual sport.

- Write down the questions you need to ask to find out the information.

- Prepare a chart where you can write in the information you hear.

# Writing folder 3

## Writing Part 9    Short message

In Part 9 of the Reading and Writing paper (Question **56**), you must write something short, like a note, an email or a postcard to a friend. You must write about three different things. Either there will be instructions giving you the three things (see Writing folder 5 on page 120), or this information will be in a message from a friend, like the task on this page.

You must write between 25 and 35 words. If you write fewer than 25 words, you will get a lower mark. You will also get a lower mark if you forget to sign your note or postcard. It is possible to get up to five marks for Part 9. Here is an example of the answer sheet for Part 9.

| Part 9 (Question 56): Write your answer below. |
| --- |
|  |
|  |
|  |
|  |
|  |

1   When you answer Part 9, you must write in
    sentences, using capital letters and full stops.
    Look at these KET answers and

- decide where the sentences should be
- correct the punctuation
- correct any other errors.

1

> I'll go to visit your town next
> friday I'd like to visit the sport
> club near your house, and I think
> it's very nice place, meet me at
> 7:00 o'clock  p.m yours

2

> I think that the more
> interesting place near my town,
> a little lake because it is not
> noisy and there are a lot of
> animals. You can drive. Love

3

> O.k. we meet in the front of the
> football ground. At 17:00 o'clock.
> I want to buy a camera and a
> computer game. See you on
> Saturday.

4

> Hello: I have a basketball, a
> football, a computer and a
> television to sell. The basketball
> and football are very new I only
> played it once. The computer and
> television were used six month.
> But I want to sell them bye

2   What needs to be added to all four answers?

3 Read the exam task below and decide what *three* things you need to write about. Underline any important words.

Read this postcard from your English friend Alex.

> Hi!
> I'm going to visit your town next month, so I have some questions for you. What's the swimming pool like? How do I get there from the town centre? When's the best time to go? Thanks for your help!
>
> Love,
> Alex

Write Alex a postcard. Answer the questions. Write **25–35** words. Write the postcard on your answer sheet.

4 Which sample answer, A or B, is better? Think about these questions.

1 How long is each answer?
2 Does the writer answer all of Alex's questions?
3 Is there enough information for Alex?

**A**
> Hi Alex
> There's a swimming pool near the motorway. Why not go at lunchtime or on Saturday? See you.
> Grazia

**B**
> Dear Alex
> It'll be nice to see you next month. The best pool is ten minutes by bus from the centre (bus number 34). The water's really warm! Swim in the morning, because it gets busy later.
> Love Juan

5 Write any extra information that is needed in the answer(s).

6 Which of Alex's questions (1–3) do sentences **A–H** answer? Write 1, 2 or 3 beside each sentence.

1 What's the swimming pool like?
2 How do I get there from the town centre?
3 When's the best time to go to the swimming pool?

A You can take a taxi from the main square. *2*
B It's 25 metres long and it's very wide.
C I'd walk – it's only fifteen minutes away.
D I think you should get there around five.
E The building's made of glass and everything's very new.
F You'll love going down the slides!
G If you go in the afternoon, I can come with you.
H Get a bike when you arrive, then you can cycle there in five minutes.

7 Now write your postcard. Remember to answer all Alex's questions and write between 25 and 35 words.

# 12.1 Family trees

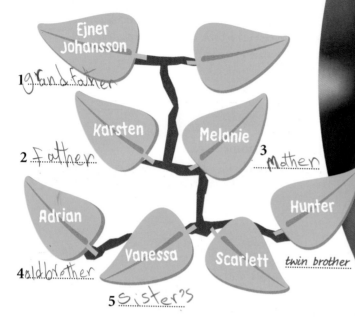

1 grandfather — Ejner Johansson

2 father — Karsten

3 Mother — Melanie

4 old brother — Adrian

5 Sister's — Vanessa

twin brother — Hunter

Scarlett

## Vocabulary

1 Read the information about Scarlett Johansson and her family. Then complete the spaces in her family tree.

> Scarlett Johansson was born on November 22 1984. She and her twin brother Hunter are the youngest of four children. Their older brother is called Adrian and their sister's name is Vanessa. Mother, Melanie, lives in Los Angeles and their father, Karsten, is in New York. Karsten is half-Danish. (Scarlett's grandfather is the famous Danish writer Ejner Johansson.)

2 Write the words for other people in a family. Some letters are given to help you.

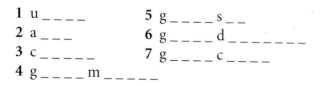

1 u _ _ _ _
2 a _ _ _
3 c _ _ _ _ _
4 g _ _ _ _ m _ _ _ _ _
5 g _ _ _ _ s _ _
6 g _ _ _ _ d _ _ _ _ _ _ _
7 g _ _ _ _ c _ _ _ _

3 Make your own family tree, which you will use later in this lesson.

## Listening

4 🎧 Listen to a girl called Helen asking Nick about their grandfather's party. For questions 1–5, tick **A**, **B** or **C**. Listen again to check your answers.

1 The party for their grandfather will be on
   **A** Friday.　**B** Saturday.　**C** Sunday.

2 Where will the party be?
   **A** at a restaurant
   **B** at a golf club
   **C** at Nick's house

3 The party will begin at
   **A** 2.45.　**B** 3.30.　**C** 4.00.

4 Who will Helen drive to the party?
   **A** Aunt Rose　**B** Uncle Jack　**C** Nick

5 Which present does Helen want to buy?
   **A** some CDs　**B** a mirror　**C** a suitcase

## GRAMMAR EXTRA — Possessive forms

Remember these forms:

| adjective | pronoun |
|-----------|---------|
| my | mine |
| your | yours |
| his | his |
| her | hers |
| our | ours |
| your | yours |
| their | theirs |

- We use a possessive adjective before a noun:

  **my** car   **your** house   **his** party

- We use a possessive pronoun after a noun, to refer back to it:

  *I can take you in my car. – Thanks, but I'll have* **mine**. (= my car)

- We usually add 's to a noun or a name to show possession:

  *granddad's party   Mario's restaurant*

5  With a partner, look at the family trees you made in exercise 3. Compare the information. Use possessive forms.

   EXAMPLES: *Your father is called ...*
   *Your brothers are older than mine.*
   *Their names are ...*

   Report back to your classmates about what you found.

   EXAMPLES: *Paul's father is called ...*
   *His brothers are older than mine.*
   *Our sisters are both older than us.*

## Pronunciation

6  Write these words in group 1 or group 2 below.

all   August   draw   house   mouth   now   or   order   out   saw   shout   town

| group 1 /aʊ/ *cow* | group 2 /ɔː/ *draw* |
|---|---|
| | |

🎧 Listen to the recording to check your answers and repeat the words.

## SPELLING SPOT — Words ending in -le

7  The word *uncle* is often spelled wrongly as *uncel* by KET students. Sort the letters below to give other words with the same -le ending.

   1  t a c l s e   (a large old building)

      _ _ _ _ _ _

   2  e c y b l c i   (this has two wheels)

      _ _ _ _ _ _ _

   3  p a e l p   (a good fruit to eat)

      _ _ _ _ _

   4  n i l g e s   (not married)

      _ _ _ _ _ _

   5  t i l l t e   (small)

      _ _ _ _ _ _

   6  p o l e p e   (men, women and children)

      _ _ _ _ _ _

# 12.2 Large and small

1. What are the good and bad things about being part of a small family or a very large family?

2. Decide which of these things may not be possible in big families.

   - being by yourself
   - playing sport with others
   - helping younger children
   - living in a big house or flat
   - keeping the place tidy
   - having a low supermarket bill
   - doing lots of washing
   - travelling cheaply
   - annoying your older brothers and sisters

## Reading

3. Read what Sam Hayden says about his big family. Which brother is he close to? Which words tell you this?

4. Now read what Sam's brother Joe says. Who does he get on well with?

Hi, my name is Sam. I am nine and I live in a family of nine. I've got five brothers and their names are David aged sixteen, Michael aged fourteen, Joe aged twelve, Jacob aged seven and Isaac aged four. I've got a little sister Naomi aged two. My mother is called Pamela and my dad is called Bernie. I live in the county of Angus, which is in Scotland. I get on quite well with my brother Michael because he is kind and helps me. I don't get on so well with my brother Joe because he is a bit annoying. I like living in a big family and I wouldn't like to change anything.

Hello, my name is Joe Hayden and I am twelve years old. My eldest brother David is sixteen and Michael is fourteen. I have three younger brothers. My little sister, who is called Naomi, is only two.

David, Michael and I are all into music, something we always enjoy. David plays the drums and Michael plays guitar, both quite loud but no one really minds. I get on well with David but not so much with my younger brothers Jacob and Sam. David, Michael and I are lucky because we all get to escape! We go to a school that is far, far away and we are only at home during the holidays.

It's good being in a big family. You can play games like football and cricket with everyone. In smaller families, this is not possible. Also, a big family means a big house, so you can always find somewhere to be by yourself. I like that sometimes.

The bad things are that you always get little kids bugging you. They can be so noisy! Everything around you is very busy and really messy, and there's lots of washing up and laundry to do. It also costs much more to go anywhere. But I prefer being in a big family.

5 Read what Joe says again. Are sentences 1–7 below 'Right' (**A**) or 'Wrong' (**B**)? If Joe doesn't tell you the answer, choose 'Doesn't say' (**C**).

1 Michael is older than Joe. *A*
2 When David and Michael play music, the others think they are too noisy.
3 Joe's school is very famous.
4 Joe comes home from school most weekends.
5 The Hayden children play more football than cricket.
6 Joe enjoys spending a bit of time alone.
7 Joe does all the washing up when he is at home.

## Grammar Pronouns

6 All the underlined words are pronouns. Complete the table.

*I am nine.*
*Michael is kind and helps me.*
*You can be by yourself.*

| subject pronouns | object pronouns | reflexive pronouns |
|---|---|---|
| I | me | .................... |
| you | ......... | yourself |
| ........, ........, it | ........, ........, it | ............., .............., itself |
| ......... | ......... | ourselves |
| ......... | ......... | .................... |
| ......... | ......... | .................... |

7 The underlined words below are also pronouns. Complete the table.

*I wouldn't like to change anything.*
*You can play games like football and cricket with everyone.*

| things | people |
|---|---|
| .................... | .................... / someone |
| .................... | anybody / .................... |
| everything | .................... / .................... |
| .................... | .................... / no one |

8 Complete the sentences with the correct pronoun from the table in exercise 7.

1 I'm really bored – there's ....._nothing_..... to do.
2 .................... is on the phone for you, Mum.
3 Why doesn't granddad remember .................... about his schooldays?
4 Have you got a minute? I want to ask you .................... .
5 There was .................... at tennis practice yesterday – only me!
6 Are you sure you've got .................... you need?
7 This is important for .................... else in the class, so listen carefully.
8 There wasn't .................... in the playground because it was raining.

9 The relative pronouns *who* and *which* give more information about someone or something earlier in the sentence.

*My little sister, who is called Naomi, is only two.*

*I live in the county of Angus, which is in Scotland.*

Complete the sentences with *who* or *which*.

1 Jonny, .................... is from New Zealand, has two brothers.
2 The two players, .................... won all their matches last year, are doing well.
3 There's some money in my bag, .................... is on the kitchen table.
4 Bono, .................... sings in the band U2, has met the Pope.
5 I go dancing every week, .................... I really enjoy.
6 The party, .................... will start at 9.00, is for my cousin's birthday.

G ⋯⋮ page 142

## Activity

### Family fun

Tomorrow, you are going to look after a family of five children, who are between two and eleven years old. Decide what activities they would enjoy and plan how to spend your day with them.

# UNITS 9–12 **Revision**

## Speaking

1 Match questions 1–8 with sentences A–H.
Then answer the questions with a partner.

EXAMPLE: *1 G*
*I think a lot of people will drive electric cars.*

1 What kind of cars will people drive in ten years' time?
2 Are you a striker or a goalkeeper?
3 What's your bedroom like?
4 Are you going to play any sport next weekend?
5 Where was your jacket made?
6 Who was the Taj Mahal designed by?
7 Can you tell me something about your last holiday?
8 Does anyone in your family make you laugh?

A My baby sister is very funny sometimes.
B We spent two weeks at the beach and I played volleyball every day.
C In Italy, I think.
D Nobody knows – but it took 20,000 people 20 years to build it!
E I can play anywhere, but I prefer being in goal.
F Yes, the school basketball team has a match on Saturday.
G I'm not sure, perhaps they'll have hydrogen, not petrol.
H It's painted purple and I've got some great posters on the walls.

## Grammar

2 Here are some errors that candidates have made in the KET exam. Correct the sentences.

1 I enjoyed to see your family.
2 I will at the station wait for you.
3 This is the best book for to learn English.
4 I think it's will cost £30.
5 You don't need to ask nobody.
6 I don't mind to get the bus to your place.
7 We can ride horses and we can fishing in the lake.
8 If anybody are interested, call this number.
9 You can coming to London by train.
10 The village is famous because it has built from three Roman emperors.

3 Complete each second sentence using the passive.

1 We sent James a letter about the skiing trip.
A letter ........*was sent*........ to James about the skiing trip.
2 A taxi took me to the airport.
I ................................ to the airport by taxi.
3 Alex showed me round the city.
I ................................ round the city by Alex.
4 Someone famous wore this silver necklace.
This silver necklace ................................ by someone famous.
5 A Greek actor wrote this song.
This song ................................ by a Greek actor.
6 Everybody in the village knows the story about the castle.
The story about the castle ................................ by everybody in the village.

# Vocabulary

**4** Complete each space in this text about football with one word. The first letter and the number of letters is given.

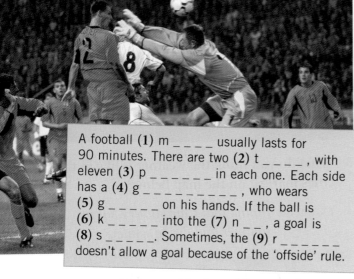

A football **(1)** m _ _ _ _ usually lasts for 90 minutes. There are two **(2)** t _ _ _ _ , with eleven **(3)** p _ _ _ _ _ _ in each one. Each side has a **(4)** g _ _ _ _ _ _ _ _ _ , who wears **(5)** g _ _ _ _ _ on his hands. If the ball is **(6)** k _ _ _ _ _ into the **(7)** n _ _ , a goal is **(8)** s _ _ _ _ _. Sometimes, the **(9)** r _ _ _ _ _ _ doesn't allow a goal because of the 'offside' rule.

**5** Decide which word is the odd one out.

1 aunt  granddaughter  cousin  mother
2 mirror  poster  bookshelf  desk
3 sofa  wardrobe  curtains  bed
4 grey  pink  red  orange
5 sailing  golf  windsurfing  swimming
6 wood  metal  silver  glass

**6** Read the sentences about a holiday. Choose the best word (**A, B** or **C**) for each space.

1 Some friends of mine .................... to visit Ireland for a week.
   **A** would       **B** enjoy       **C** want

2 I'm .................... during that week and I'm going to go with them.
   **A** empty       **B** free       **C** ready

3 We're going to take our bikes so we can go .................... .
   **A** walking       **B** cycling       **C** driving

4 We won't take much .................... with us, but we'll need to carry a tent.
   **A** luggage       **B** suitcase       **C** bags

5 We'll .................... a campsite by a lake and go swimming if the weather's good.
   **A** look       **B** find       **C** arrive

# Writing

**7** Correct the punctuation in these emails. Then say which email answers each question below. One question does not match any of the emails.

**A**

To:
From:
Subject:

Id love to come sailing with you and your family andrea I go sailing about ten times a year so ive got something to wear can I borrow a life jacket

**B**

To:
From:
Subject:

You asked me about my room well its quite big with two windows from one i can only see the street but from the other theres a lovely park with trees i want some new curtains for my room

**C**

To:
From:
Subject:

Im going to sicily with my brother at easter were going to spend a week by the sea and then well go walking near etna its beautiful there

1 How big is your bedroom?
2 Where do you think you'll go?
3 Are you good at sailing?
4 Why will you be late?
5 When are you going to have a holiday?
6 Is there anything you'd like for your room?
7 What will you do there?
8 Would you like to come on our boat next weekend?
9 What can you see from your window?
10 Will you need any special clothes?

# 13.1 Sun, rain or snow?

## Vocabulary

1 Find nine weather words in the word square
(→ ↓ and ↑) and complete the sentences
below. The first one has been done for you.

| d | u | r | w | e | t | y |
|---|---|---|---|---|---|---|
| r | p | a | s | y | o | s |
| y | w | i | n | d | y | t |
| g | y | n | o | u | n | o |
| g | e | i | w | o | n | r |
| o | o | n | y | l | u | m |
| f | r | g | y | c | s | y |

1 It's very w _i_ _n_ _d_ y today – let's fly our kites.
2 It's r _ _ _ _ _ g in Bogotá at the moment.
3 It's a lovely s _ _ _ y day for a bike ride.
4 It's c _ _ _ _ y so we can't go to the beach.
5 It's w _ t when the monsoon starts.
6 It's very f _ _ _ y outside – I can't see far.
7 It gets very s _ _ _ _ y in the mid-west of the
USA in summer.
8 It's d _ y at the moment so let's go for a walk.
9 It was s _ _ _ y when I went to Beijing in
January.

2 What's the weather like where you live ...
... today?   ... in December?   ... in July?

Which is the hottest / coldest / wettest / driest
place in your country?

3 What do you think the weather is like in the
cities marked on the map below?

EXAMPLE: *I think that Cairo is very hot in
summer and dry in winter.*

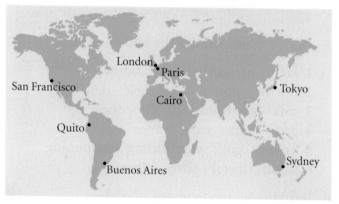

## Listening

4 🎧 Listen to Dan talking about his round-the-
world trip with a friend.

What was the weather like in each place? Match
the places (1–5) with the weather (A–H).

EXAMPLE:
0 London  *D*

1 Paris
2 Cairo
3 Sydney
4 Tokyo
5 San Francisco

A cloud
B fog
C ice
D rain
E snow
F sun
G thunderstorm
H wind

## GRAMMAR EXTRA
*(not) as ... as*

- On the recording Dan said:
  *It **wasn't as** hot **as** in summer.*
  This means that Cairo is hotter in summer.

  *It **wasn't as** expensive **as** Tokyo.*
  This means that Tokyo was more expensive than Sydney.

- When we compare things that are the same, we can use:
  *the same as*   *The weather today is **the same as** yesterday.*

  *as ... as*   *It's **as** cold today **as** it was yesterday.*

5 With a partner, talk about the weather report below. Use *(not) as ... as, the same as ...* or a comparative adjective + *than*.

   EXAMPLES:
   *The weather in Athens yesterday was not as hot as in Delhi.*
   *The weather in Rio de Janeiro was rainy, the same as in Tokyo.*
   *Madrid was colder than Mexico City.*

### Around the World Yesterday

| | | |
|---|---|---|
| Athens | 15° | r |
| Beijing | 7° | cl |
| Delhi | 34° | s |
| Madrid | 15° | cl |
| Mexico City | 23° | s |
| Moscow | −1° | sn |
| Rio de Janeiro | 29° | r |
| Rome | 13° | cl |
| Sydney | 22° | cl |
| Tokyo | 10° | r |
| Vancouver | 6° | sn |

cl = cloudy    r = rainy    s = sunny    sn = snowy

## Pronunciation

6  **What words are missing from these sentences?**

   1 You went .............. Paris.
   2 Paris was .............. bit cloudy.
   3 We had .............. great time.
   4 I'd love .............. go there.
   5 We stayed in .............. hotel.
   6 We did ............. shopping there.
   7 There was no rain .............. all.
   8 It was warmer ............. some of the other places.

   🎧 **Listen to check your answers. What do the missing words have in common?**

7  **Read these sentences about a camping trip. Underline the unstressed words which have the sound /ə/.**

   1 Bob went camping with a friend.
   2 Both of them like camping.
   3 They got to the campsite late.
   4 They slept for ten hours.
   5 They had eggs for breakfast.
   6 They had hot chocolate to drink.
   7 There was a wonderful view from their tent.
   8 Bob took some great photos.

   🎧 **Listen to check your answers.**

## 1 True or false?

1 In Libya, in 1922, the temperature reached 57.8 degrees centigrade. It was <u>hot enough</u> to fry an egg on the road!

2 It's <u>too dangerous</u> to go outside if there is a tornado. People in parts of the USA have a special 'safe' room to go to, usually under the ground.

3 It's very dry in the Atacama Desert in Chile. It only gets 15 mm of rain a year. It's <u>too dry</u> to grow anything.

4 There are more tornadoes every year in the UK than anywhere else in the world. They are usually <u>not big enough</u> to worry about.

## Grammar *enough* and *too*

- Look at the underlined phrases above:
  adjective + *enough* — *hot enough*
  *too* + adjective — *too dangerous*

- We can also use *to* + infinitive after these:
  adjective + *enough* – *hot enough to fry an egg*
  *too* + adjective – *too dangerous to go outside*

**G** ···> page 142

## 2 With a partner, look at the pictures and decide what each person is saying.

1 *It's too cold to go swimming.*

## 3 Complete these sentences using *too* or *enough*, plus one of the adjectives and one of the verbs.

| adjectives | verbs |
|---|---|
| windy | to see |
| cold | to switch on |
| cloudy | ~~to go out~~ |
| ~~wet~~ | to walk |
| icy | to wear |
| foggy | to lie |
| hot | to see |

1 It was ........*too wet to go out*........ without an umbrella.

2 It wasn't ...................................... on the beach, so we went to the cinema.

3 It was ...................................... where we were going in the car.

4 It's ...................................... any stars in the sky tonight.

5 It isn't ...................................... the heating in the evenings.

6 It's ...................................... a hat – it will blow away.

7 It was ...................................... to school.

## Reading

**4** Read this article about a man called Warren Faidley, who has an unusual job. Choose the best word, **A**, **B** or **C**, for each space.

| | | | |
|---|---|---|---|
| **0** | **A** an | **B** a | **C** the |
| **1** | **A** is | **B** was | **C** were |
| **2** | **A** most | **B** more | **C** lots |
| **3** | **A** When | **B** Where | **C** Because |
| **4** | **A** by | **B** of | **C** at |
| **5** | **A** took | **B** take | **C** taking |
| **6** | **A** too | **B** very | **C** enough |
| **7** | **A** can | **B** must | **C** have |
| **8** | **A** something | **B** nothing | **C** everything |

# The man who loves tornadoes

Warren Faidley has **(0)** ......... unusual job – he likes bad weather so much that he follows storms, really bad storms like tornadoes. He **(1)** ......... born in the middle of the USA. This part of the world has **(2)** ......... tornadoes than the rest of the country. Warren travels all over North America to find tornadoes and other storms. **(3)** ......... he finds one he makes a film **(4)** ......... it and uses his computer to give him extra information. He says he enjoys **(5)** ......... photos of bad weather. He believes it is **(6)** ......... important for people to know about bad weather. He works for the government and also for Hollywood. He helped on the film *Twister*, which was about tornadoes. He says his job **(7)** ......... be very frightening but he does **(8)** ......... he needs to do to keep himself safe.

## SPELLING SPOT — *to*, *too* and *two*

Be careful with the spelling of *to*, *too* and *two*.

**5** Complete the sentences with the correct word.

**1** I went ............... Tokyo last year for ............... weeks.

**2** My cousin went ............... .

**3** We took taxis ............... places because it was ............... difficult for us ............... use the subway.

**4** When I got home I tried ............... cook some Japanese food.

**5** I made some sushi and invited ............... friends for a meal.

**6** They wanted ............... know how ............... make it so they could cook it ............... .

**6** Here are some errors that candidates have made in the KET exam. Correct the sentences.

**1** The weather are very sunny.

**2** This year the weather colder than last year.

**3** What does the weather like in Australia?

**4** The weather in Caracas is hotter as in Santiago.

**5** It was not enough hot to go swimming.

**6** I like sunny weather too much.

## Activity

### Seasons

- Get into four teams, one for each season: spring, summer, autumn and winter.
- Take it in turns each to say a sentence about your season, for example:
  *In winter I like being inside where it is warm and cosy.*
- The team scores a point for each correct sentence.
- The team with the most points is the winner.
- Write a paragraph about your favourite season and also say why you don't like other seasons as much.

# Exam folder 7

## Listening Part 2    Multiple matching

In Part 2 of the Listening paper there are five questions (**6–10**) and a choice of eight answers (**A–H**). There are always two speakers (usually two friends). You must choose which of **A–H** answers questions **6–10**. There is an example first to help you.

**6–10** are usually names, days of the week, months, etc. and **A–H** are usually topics, for example sports, presents, rooms, etc.

1   Give a title to each of the following topic sets and add as many words as you can.

    **1** Monday, Tuesday ... *Days of the week – Wednesday, Thursday, ...*
    **2** January, February ...
    **3** football, swimming ...
    **4** blue, red ...
    **5** dress, jacket ...
    **6** aunt, sister ...
    **7** apples, soup ...

2   Look at the exam task on the opposite page. Here is the first part of the recording script. It is possible to divide it into sections.

*Introduction*
**Girl:** Hi, Nick.
**Boy:** Hi, Penny. How was your holiday in Switzerland?

*The example – Nick*
**Girl:** It was great – hot and sunny every day and some nice shops!
Look, Nick, I bought you a cup. See, it's got 'Switzerland' written on it.

*First question – James*
**Boy:** Oh, thanks! Did you get a pen for James? He's always taking mine.
**Girl:** I got him a CD of a local band – he likes anything to do with music.

In the example you usually hear just one object mentioned, but for the questions you may hear one or two. You must listen carefully to make sure you choose the correct answer. In question 6, both 'pen' and 'CD' are mentioned. CD is the correct answer.

## Exam advice

*Before you listen*
- Read the questions and answers very carefully.
- The questions, 6–10, will be in the order in which you hear them.

*First listening*
- If there are two things mentioned (objects, places, days, etc.), think about which is the correct answer. Write down both words or letters next to the number if you aren't sure.

*Second listening*
- Check your choice of answer is correct.
- At the end of the Listening test, copy your answers onto your answer sheet. Opposite is an example of the answer sheet for Part 2.

**Part 2**

| | A | B | C | D | E | F | G | H |
|---|---|---|---|---|---|---|---|---|
| 6 | ☐ | ☐ | ☐ | ☐ | ☐ | ☐ | ☐ | ☐ |
| 7 | ☐ | ☐ | ☐ | ☐ | ☐ | ☐ | ☐ | ☐ |
| 8 | ☐ | ☐ | ☐ | ☐ | ☐ | ☐ | ☐ | ☐ |
| 9 | ☐ | ☐ | ☐ | ☐ | ☐ | ☐ | ☐ | ☐ |
| 10 | ☐ | ☐ | ☐ | ☐ | ☐ | ☐ | ☐ | ☐ |

---

## Part 2

### Questions 6–10

Listen to Penny talking to her cousin about the presents she bought on holiday for her friends.
Who got which present?

For questions **6–10**, write a letter (**A–H**) next to each person.
You will hear the conversation twice.

**Example:**

**0** Nick    **D**

---

| **People** | | **Presents** |
|---|---|---|
| **6** James | ☐ | **A** book |
| **7** Becky | ☐ | **B** CD |
| **8** Alice | ☐ | **C** comb |
| **9** Tom | ☐ | **D** cup |
| **10** Lucy | ☐ | **E** pen |
| | | **F** picture |
| | | **G** soap |
| | | **H** watch |

## Reading

1 Do this questionnaire with a partner and decide who likes reading the most.

2 Read the photo story below. Do you like this type of story?

With a partner, talk about how you think the story will end.

**1** How many books do you read each year?
- A fewer than 5
- B 6–20
- C more than 20

**2** Where do you read?
- A at the beach
- B in my bedroom
- C in the bath

**3** What kind of books do you like?
- A picture books /comics
- B love stories
- C adventure stories
- D books that make you laugh
- E detective stories
- F science fiction books

Who reads the most in the class? Which type of book is the most popular in your class?

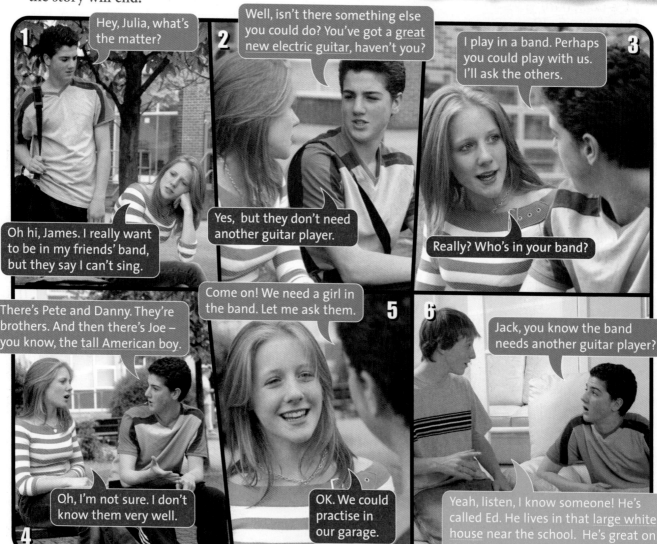

**1** Hey, Julia, what's the matter?

Oh hi, James. I really want to be in my friends' band, but they say I can't sing.

**2** Well, isn't there something else you could do? You've got a great new electric guitar, haven't you?

Yes, but they don't need another guitar player.

**3** I play in a band. Perhaps you could play with us. I'll ask the others.

Really? Who's in your band?

**4** There's Pete and Danny. They're brothers. And then there's Joe – you know, the tall American boy.

Oh, I'm not sure. I don't know them very well.

Come on! We need a girl in the band. Let me ask them.

**5** OK. We could practise in our garage.

**6** Jack, you know the band needs another guitar player?

Yeah, listen, I know someone! He's called Ed. He lives in that large white house near the school. He's great on the guitar and he writes songs!

# Grammar  Position of adjectives

- If there is more than one adjective before a noun, they are put in a special order. For example, opinion (e.g. *nice*) is before fact (e.g. *old*).

  We say *nice old house* NOT *nice and old house*.

3  Complete this chart with the words underlined in the photo story.

| 1<br>What's it like?<br>*opinion* | 2<br>How big?<br>*size* | 3<br>How old?<br>*age* | 4<br>What colour? | 5<br>Where's it from?<br>*nationality* | 6<br>What kind? | NOUN |
|---|---|---|---|---|---|---|
| | | | | | | guitar |
| | | | | | | boy |
| | | | | | | house |

4  Put these words in the right order.

1  a book boring old
2  a magazine colourful new
3  a computer modern Japanese
4  the library new school excellent
5  the book long adventure
6  the bag expensive leather little
7  a dress beautiful white
8  a writer young clever

**G** ┄┄┊ page 143

5  With a partner, describe the following:

EXAMPLE:
*My school is an attractive, modern building and I have interesting, young teachers. There is also an expensive, new science block.*

1  your school
2  your favourite book
3  your favourite item of clothing
4  your best friend
5  your bedroom

## Pronunciation

6  All these words from the photo story have a silent consonant. Draw a circle round the silent letter in each of them.

1  ⓦrites      2  know       3  white
4  what's      5  listen      6  who

🎧 Listen to check.

7  All the silent letters are missing in the words below. Match the silent letter with the right word so the spelling is correct.

| t | n | h | ~~s~~ | b | k | d | l |
|---|---|---|---|---|---|---|---|

1  i s̲ land      2  cas _ le      3  ha _ f          4  clim _
5  autum _      6  _ nife        7  We _ nesday      8  _ our

🎧 With a partner, say the words and then listen to check.

---

**SPELLING SPOT**    ( Words that are often confused )

*buy – by – Bye*
*whether – weather*
*things – thinks*
*want – won't*
*bed – bad*

8  Complete these sentences with the correct word.

1  ................. the time she is 20 she will know ................................ she ................. to be a doctor or a teacher.
2  The ................................ was really ................. when I was on holiday.
3  You don't ................. to stay in ................. all day, do you?
4  She said '.................' and went out to ................. a book.
5  We are going to get some ................................ from town.
6  I ................................ be home late tonight.

## Vocabulary

1 Put these school subjects in order. Tell your partner why.
1 = You like this subject best.
8 = You like this subject least.

| | |
|---|---|
| maths | |
| history | |
| languages | |
| sport | |
| art | |
| geography | |
| music | |
| science | |

2 Is there any subject you would like to do but can't do at your school?
Tell your partner.

## Listening

3 🎧 Sylvia is 14 and wants to be an actor. You will hear her asking for information about Saturday morning classes at a theatre school in London.
Listen and write the missing information.

Theatre School
0 Day: saturday
1 Date of new classes: 3rd ....................
2 Send cheque for:     £....................
3 Time classes begin:     ....................
4 Address: .................................... High street
5 Best bus to get:     ....................

4 Match sentences 1–4 from Sylvia's conversation with responses A–D.

1 Can I help you?
2 Could I visit the school to see what it's like?
3 When can I come and visit?
4 Thank you very much.

A Not at all.
B Any time.
C Yes, please.
D Of course.

🎧 Listen again to check your answers.

5 Now do the same with 1–10 and A–J.

1 I can't come swimming tomorrow afternoon.
2 Ouch! You stood on my foot!
3 Can I have a kilo of tomatoes, please?
4 I've passed all my exams.
5 Would you mind opening the window?
6 Would you like a drink?
7 Hi! How are you?
8 Hi! Is that Sally speaking?
9 Can I sit here?
10 Let's go to the cinema.

A Fine, thanks.
B Sorry I can't. I'm busy.
C I'm afraid it's taken.
D No, it's Lisa.
E I'm so sorry!
F Not at all.
G It doesn't matter.
H Congratulations!
I That'll be £1.50.
J Nothing for me, thanks.

🎧 Listen to check your answers.

6 Complete the crossword.

**Across**

3 French is an example of this.
4 You can get books from this place.
6 The teacher writes on this.
7 You must do this when the teacher is talking.
9 The person who teaches you.
11 You study this to know about the past.
13 You do this after school.

**Down**

1 You write with this.
2 What you do at school.
5 You put books on this.
8 You sit at this in class.
10 A place to keep things in.
12 Past simple of *see*.

Sylvia says: *Can I get a bus rather than come by car?*

7 Write sentences that are true for you using these words.

1 tennis / volleyball
prefer / play
*I prefer to play tennis rather than volleyball.*

2 maths / English
prefer / study

3 book / TV
prefer / read / watch

4 English / Japanese
would like / learn

5 football / sing
would prefer / play / learn

6 guitar / piano
would like / play

7 teacher / doctor
would prefer / be

8 Australia / the USA
would prefer / live

9 someone rich / poor
would like / marry

10 Brad Pitt / Jennifer Lopez
would like / meet

**Activity**

• In groups, talk about your school. First of all, talk about what the school is like now. Talk about the building, the subjects you study, the classrooms, etc.

• Now talk about the changes you want to make. You can change the length of the school day, the types of lessons you have – anything!

• When you have finished, make a presentation to the rest of the class. You can use drawings if you want to.

# Exam folder 8

## Reading Part 3    Multiple choice

Part 3 of the Reading and Writing paper tests the type of English you use every day in conversation. Part 3 is divided into two parts:

Questions **11–15** have five multiple-choice questions and one example.
Questions **16–20** are based on a conversation and contain five matching items and one example. You must choose your answer from eight possible answers.

### Exam advice

- For questions **11–15**, think about where or when you would say each question or statement.
- For questions **16–20**, read through the instructions and the example, as they will tell you what the conversation is about.
- Make sure you read the whole conversation before you choose your answers.
- Cross out the example letter so that you don't choose it again by accident.
- Be careful not to choose an answer just because it uses the same words as the question.
- Check your answers carefully when you transfer them to your answer sheet. An example of the answer sheet for Part 3 is on the page opposite.

---

**Part 3**

**Questions 11–15**

Complete the five conversations.
For questions **11–15**, mark **A**, **B** or **C** on your answer sheet.

**Example:**
0

What do you do?

A I'm studying.

B I'm a doctor.

C I'll see you tomorrow.

*Answer:* 0   A B C

---

**11** Can I help you?

     **A** Not at all.
     **B** You're welcome.
     **C** Yes, can I pay for this here?

**12** Are you ready?

     **A** I agree.
     **B** Not yet!
     **C** Here it is!

**13** Where's the bus stop?

    **A** It's over there.
    **B** Nowhere.
    **C** I don't mind.

**14** It's hot in here.

    **A** That's fine.
    **B** Yes, isn't it?
    **C** Let's open it.

**15** That'll be £3.98, please.

    **A** Here you are.
    **B** I'm afraid I can't.
    **C** That's nice.

**Part 3**

| | A B C | | A B C D E F G H |
|---|---|---|---|
| **11** | ☐ ☐ ☐ | **16** | ☐ ☐ ☐ ☐ ☐ ☐ ☐ ☐ |
| **12** | ☐ ☐ ☐ | **17** | ☐ ☐ ☐ ☐ ☐ ☐ ☐ ☐ |
| **13** | ☐ ☐ ☐ | **18** | ☐ ☐ ☐ ☐ ☐ ☐ ☐ ☐ |
| **14** | ☐ ☐ ☐ | **19** | ☐ ☐ ☐ ☐ ☐ ☐ ☐ ☐ |
| **15** | ☐ ☐ ☐ | **20** | ☐ ☐ ☐ ☐ ☐ ☐ ☐ ☐ |

**Questions 16–20**

Complete the conversation between two friends.
What does Jenny say to Marco?

For questions **16–20**, mark the correct letter **A–H** on your answer sheet.

**Example:**

*Marco:* Who's your favourite writer, Jenny?

*Jenny:* **0** ...................

*Answer:* **0** | A B C D E F G H | ☐ ☐ ☐ ☐ ☐ ☐ ■ ☐ |

---

*Marco:* Oh, yes. I love all her Harry Potter books.

*Jenny:* **16** ...................

*Marco:* You'll have to wait for a while, I think.

*Jenny:* **17** ...................

*Marco:* Have you seen the latest Harry Potter film?

*Jenny:* **18** ...................

*Marco:* My brother says it's even better than the others.

*Jenny:* **19** ...................

*Marco:* That's a good idea. When are you free?

*Jenny:* **20** ...................

*Marco:* That's great. See you then.

**A** I know. I read somewhere that she hasn't started writing it yet.

**B** It's a book I'm reading at the moment.

**C** What about going to see it together?

**D** Me too! I can't wait to read the next one.

**E** I got it last Saturday.

**F** Friday is best because I don't have any homework.

**G** I think it must be J.K. Rowling.

**H** Not yet. I've been quite busy.

## FAMOUS FOR
# FIFTEEN

Jamie Oliver is Britain's most famous chef. He made his first TV cooking programmes when he was only 23, got married at 25 and was given a special award by the Queen at 28. A top supermarket pays to use him in their advertisements, he sells almost as many books as J.K. Rowling, and journalists are always writing articles about him.

Jamie has also opened the restaurant *Fifteen* in London. The name doesn't describe where the restaurant is – it's because he chose this number of young people to become cooks there. Not one of them knew how to cook so Jamie sent them to college in the year before he opened the restaurant. They also visited other restaurants to learn more.

*Fifteen* really started because of a conversation Jamie had with his wife's friend. She worked with difficult children and found that they always enjoyed cooking, so Jamie decided to start a restaurant business to help young people with problems.

Jamie is at the restaurant five days a week but always spends weekends with his wife and children. He says he has never been happier and only wants to go on cooking. He works hard but pays himself nothing, because all the money is used to train new students every six months. Today, 85 people work at *Fifteen*, many more than when it first opened. The restaurant is always full and Jamie has four receptionists answering more than 3000 phone calls a day from customers wanting to book a table!

**1** Match these jobs to photos a–e.

chef   farmer   journalist   nurse   receptionist

**2** Now match each job to its description.

**1** looks after those who are ill
**2** works outside in all kinds of weather
**3** helps people on the phone
**4** makes good things to eat
**5** finds out interesting information

## Reading

**3** Read the article and answer the questions. The colours show you the right part of the text.

**1** At the age of 23, Jamie Oliver
  A  got married.
  B  went on television.
  C  met the Queen.

**2** Now, Jamie Oliver
  A  is the top-selling writer in Britain.
  B  writes articles for several newspapers.
  C  does some work for a supermarket.

**3** Jamie's restaurant is called *Fifteen* because of
  A  the first staff there.
  B  the opening hours.
  C  the street number.

**4** The cooks who joined *Fifteen*
  A  came from other restaurants.
  B  had no training in cooking.
  C  were already at a college.

**5** The idea for *Fifteen* came from
  A  Jamie.
  B  Jamie's wife.
  C  a friend of Jamie's wife.

**6** Jamie would like to
  A  have more weekends at home.
  B  spend less time cooking.
  C  do just what he is doing now.

**7** How is *Fifteen* different now?
  A  It has more staff than it did.
  B  It no longer trains any students.
  C  It is less busy than it was.

## Grammar   Present perfect

4  Question 7 could say: *How <u>has</u> Fifteen <u>changed</u> recently?*

The possible answers could be:
*The number of staff **has grown**.*
*Only trained cooks **have found** jobs there.*
*The restaurant **hasn't been** so busy.*

These are all examples of the present perfect. How is it formed?

5  When is the present perfect used? Choose **A** or **B** for sentences **1–4**.

**A** something that started in the past but is still true in the present
**B** something that happened recently (we aren't told when)

1  Jamie Oliver has written a new book.
2  Jamie Oliver has always enjoyed cooking.
3  *Fifteen* has been full every night.
4  I've booked a table at *Fifteen* for your birthday.

Be careful! You cannot say: *I've booked a table two hours ago.* Which tense should you use here? Why?

Which sentence (5–7) is not correct? Why? Choose **A** or **B** for the other two sentences.

5  *Fifteen* has been open for two years.
6  *Fifteen* has opened in 2003.
7  *Fifteen* has been open since 2003.

**G** ···⟶ page 143

6  Correct any errors with verbs in these sentences. Some sentences are correct.

1  Jamie Oliver has made a new TV programme.
2  His books have sold well for several years.
3  The supermarket has advertised for more staff last week.
4  I haven't been to this restaurant since August.
5  Marion has become a doctor in 2002.
6  Have you always worked from home?
7  Lee has arrived for his meeting an hour ago.
8  The company has opened offices in different parts of Spain.

7  Put the verbs in brackets into the present perfect or the past simple.

Tom Stone works in south-east England as an engineer. Two years ago, he **(1)** ......*bought*...... (buy) a house in France and **(2)** ........................ (move) there with his family. Both his children like their French schools and they **(3)** ........................ (make) lots of new friends. For two years, Tom **(4)** ........................ (travel) to work every day on Le Shuttle, a train that takes cars to England. When he **(5)** ........................ (begin) doing this journey, he **(6)** ........................ (decide) to catch the train at 5 am. This **(7)** ........................ (mean) leaving his house at 3.30 am! Tom **(8)** ..................... (be + not) sure about doing this every day, but says he soon **(9)** ........................ (find) it easy to get up early. He **(10)** ........................ (take) the same train ever since, because then he can be home again by 6 pm.

8  Have you ever ...

... met a chef?          ... seen a famous person?
... been to hospital?    ... wanted to be rich?

Now ask and answer the questions above, and add one of the questions below.

| | |
|---|---|
| Why? | What did you do? |
| Why not? | Who did you meet/see? |
| When was that? | |

**SPELLING SPOT**                              -er / -or

Many words for jobs end in -*er*, e.g. *teacher*, but a few end in -*or*, e.g. *inventor*.

9  Read the descriptions of some jobs. What is the word for each one? The first letter is already there. What is the job in the yellow box?

1  This person uses a camera.
2  Ask this person to change the colour of your walls.
3  This person works for a newspaper.
4  You will find this person in a theatre.
5  See this person if you are feeling ill.

1  p _ _ _ _ _ _ _ _ _ _
2              p _ _ _ _ _ _
3     j _ _ _ _ _ _ _ _ _
4           a _ _ _ _
5           d _ _ _ _ _

THE NEWS

1 Have you ever wanted to get a job in the evenings or at weekends? Why? / Why not?

2 Answer these questions about the job advertisements by choosing **A**, **B** or **C**.

  1 Which job is only for one day a week?
  2 Which job can you do if you are only 13?
  3 Which job pays nothing?

---

**A**

**Paper boys/girls wanted**
Hours 6–8 am and 5–6 pm
Must have own bike and
be 13 or older
£4.50 per day, more at
weekends

---

**B**
**Extra help needed on Saturdays ...**
... in our busy music shop
(open 10–6)
Suitable for student 16+
Get special prices on our CDs!
Good hourly pay

---

**C** **Do you care about the elderly?**
Then help our staff at Sunnydale Old People's Home.
We can't pay you but you'll find your visits good fun!
Play games, read stories, or just talk to an elderly
person – it's your choice.
If you are over 14 and have a few hours a week free
after school or at weekends, phone us now on
0124 426638.

---

3 Would you ever work for no money?
Why? / Why not?

---

## GRAMMAR EXTRA    *just* and *yet*

These words are often used with the present perfect.

- *Just* means that something has happened very recently.
   > I've **just** got a new job.
   > Have you **just** arrived?

- *Yet* means that something hasn't happened but will happen soon.
   > Carmen hasn't taken her driving test **yet**.
   > Haven't you done your homework **yet**?

4 Write out the sentences and complete them with *just* or *yet* and the present perfect of the verb in brackets. Remember to make the verb negative with *yet*.

EXAMPLES:
Isabel (finish) her nursing course. ✓
*Isabel has just finished her nursing course.*
Isabel (finish) her nursing course. ✗
*Isabel hasn't finished her nursing course yet.*

1 The receptionist at the sports centre (leave) a message for you. ✓
2 Tom (meet) his new boss. ✗
3 They (send) me any information about the job. ✗
4 The newsagent (stop) using paper boys and girls. ✓
5 My uncle (give) me a job in his café. ✓
6 Charlotte and Andy (find) a photographer for their wedding. ✗
7 I (choose) a computer course to go on. ✓
8 The supermarket manager (pay) Mike for his extra hours. ✗

# Listening

5 Before you listen, spend 20 seconds reading the questions below.

🎧 Listen to Sam phoning Kate Richards about a Saturday job at her music shop. For questions 1–5, tick **A**, **B** or **C**.

1 The hours for the Saturday job are
   A 8 am – 8 pm.
   B 9 am – 7 pm.
   C 10 am – 6 pm.

2 The job will be mainly
   A adding up money.
   B cleaning the shop.
   C serving customers.

3 How much can Sam earn when he starts?
   A £5.25 an hour
   B £6.30 an hour
   C £7.00 an hour

4 Where is the music shop?
   A near the university
   B in the centre of town
   C across the river from Sam's home

5 Which day will Sam visit the shop?
   A Wednesday
   B Thursday
   C Friday

# Pronunciation

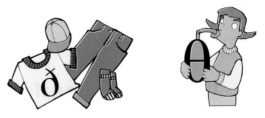

6 🎧 You will hear these sentences from the recorded conversation in exercise 5 again. Listen carefully to the underlined and circled sounds because they are different.

A: <u>Th</u>at's true. Well, any o<u>th</u>er questions?
B: How about (Th)ursday or Friday?

🎧 Say the words aloud. Then listen to and repeat some more words and write them in group 1 or group 2.

| group 1 /ð/ *that, other* | group 2 /θ/ *Thursday* |
|---|---|
|  |  |
|  |  |
|  |  |

7 🎧 Now listen to sentences **1–6** twice. Underline any ð sound the first time you listen. Circle any θ sound the next time.

1 I've worked for the last two months in my father's shop.
2 Let's look at all these job adverts together.
3 I thought you were working at the museum. Have you finished there?
4 Jenny, thanks for looking through my article.
5 That footballer earns a hundred and thirty thousand euros a month!
6 My brother's just got a job in the north of Sweden.

## Activity

### 101 jobs

- Get into groups of three or four.
- Your teacher will write the names of some places on the board. Write down as many different jobs as you can for each place.

EXAMPLE:
*school:* secretary, teacher, receptionist, gardener, cook, cleaner

# Writing folder 4

## Writing Part 8    Information transfer

In Part 8 of the Reading and Writing paper you must copy information from two texts onto a form or a set of notes. There are five spaces (**51–55**) to complete. The information will come from both texts.

1   Look at these texts and say what each one is.

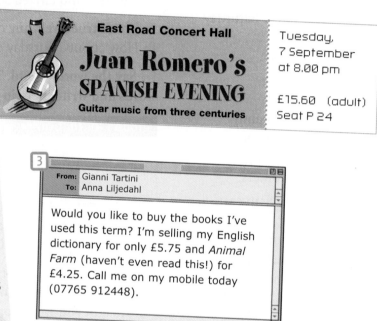

**1** East Road Concert Hall
**Juan Romero's SPANISH EVENING**
Guitar music from three centuries
Tuesday, 7 September at 8.00 pm
£15.60 (adult)
Seat P 24

**2** Summer Shakespeare Season
**Must finish August 29!**
**ALL'S WELL THAT ENDS WELL**
Enjoy this famous play outside, in the beautiful gardens of Brenton College
Tickets on sale at Ardingley Theatre, New Street
£21 with welcome drink, £18.75 ticket only (£12.30 with college card)

**3**
From: Gianni Tartini
To: Anna Liljedahl

Would you like to buy the books I've used this term? I'm selling my English dictionary for only £5.75 and *Animal Farm* (haven't even read this!) for £4.25. Call me on my mobile today (07765 912448).

2   Find the following information in the texts. Be careful to copy everything correctly.

1 Phone number: .....................................................
2 Name of book: .....................................................
3 Last date to see play: .....................................................
4 Name of guitar player: .....................................................
5 Student ticket price: .....................................................
6 Time of concert: .....................................................
7 Where to see play: .....................................................
8 Price of dictionary: .....................................................

## Exam advice

- Read both texts quickly to find out the topic.
- Look at the notes or form (questions **51–55**).
- Decide if each space needs a number or word(s).
- Read the texts again carefully to find the answers.
- Write all your answers on the question paper first.
- Don't write more than you need to.
- Write any numbers in figures, not words.
- Check your copying of numbers carefully.
- Check spelling and use of capital letters in names, days of the week, months, etc.
- Write your answers on your answer sheet. Opposite is an example of the answer sheet for Part 8.

| Part 8 | | Do not write here |
|---|---|---|
| 51 | | 1 41 2 ☐ ☐ |
| 52 | | 1 42 2 ☐ ☐ |
| 53 | | 1 43 2 ☐ ☐ |
| 54 | | 1 44 2 ☐ ☐ |
| 55 | | 1 45 2 ☐ ☐ |

**Part 8**

**Questions 51–55**

Read all the information about holiday jobs in Britain.
Fill in Laura's form.
For questions **51–55**, write the information on your answer sheet.

### AU PAIR JOBS IN BRITAIN

Welcoming families in Derby (close to beautiful hills) and Eastbourne (by the sea).

Start dates 16/23/30 June

If you are 18 or over, complete our form today – you only pay £60 (£40 if you worked last summer).

---

**From:** Hana Stankova hanastan@scworld.com
**To:** Laura Tournier lauratou@free.fr

Thanks for the job advert. We're both just old enough! I can begin on June 23 too. Choose the town near the beach like me! Good luck.

---

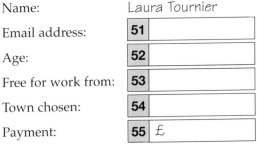

### FORM FOR AU PAIR, ENGLAND

| | |
|---|---|
| Name: | Laura Tournier |
| Email address: | **51** |
| Age: | **52** |
| Free for work from: | **53** |
| Town chosen: | **54** |
| Payment: | **55** £ |

1 Decide if these sentences about transport are true or false.

London Heathrow is the largest airport in the world.

A man in Canada put wheels on his wife's bed and cycled her to work as she slept.

If you put all the railways in the USA end to end, they would go round the world six times.

In 1783 in France, the first hot-air balloon passengers were a sheep, a duck and a snake.

## Vocabulary

2 Put the letters in the right order to spell different kinds of transport.

| | | | |
|---|---|---|---|
| 1 a i t n r | 2 h c a o c | 3 y c c b l i e | 4 t a b o |
| 5 e l a p n | 6 x t i a | 7 c t e i h p e r o l | 8 s r h e o |

3 Match each picture to a word from exercise 2. Can you add any more transport words?

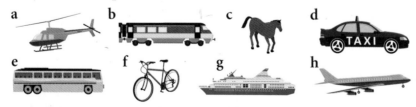

4 Now match these verbs to each kind of transport in exercise 2. Most verbs go with more than one type of transport.

board   catch   drive   fly   get   get off
get on   park   ride   sail   take off

EXAMPLE: board – *a coach, train, plane, helicopter, boat*

## Grammar  Modal verbs 2

5 What is the difference between these two examples? Which girl can choose what she does?

1 You should take the train because it's quicker than the bus.

2 You must go to Gate 43 by six o'clock.

What is the difference in meaning between the two sentences below?

3 You mustn't go to Gate 43 later than six o'clock.

4 You don't have to go to Gate 43 before six o'clock.

6 Complete the text using *should, must, mustn't* and *don't have to*. Use each verb once only.

All passengers for Jetaway's flight JT 845 to Dublin (1) ............................ go to Desk 44 in Area B. If you only have one piece of hand luggage, you (2) ............................ check it in. However, your hand luggage (3) ............................ be no larger than 55 x 40 x 20 cm and (4) ............................ weigh over 10 kg.

7 Now look at these examples. Which modal verbs in exercise 6 are closest in meaning to the underlined verbs?

1 You <u>need to</u> stay with your luggage at all times.
2 You <u>needn't</u> show your passport again until you board the plane.

**G** ···⟫ page 144

8 Read the notices and circle the correct modal verb in the sentences below.

> **Please have enough change ready for the bus driver**

1 You *needn't / need to* give the driver the correct money.

> **CARS BOARDING NOW (FOOT PASSENGERS MAY STAY IN LOUNGE)**

2 If you aren't driving, you *should / needn't* get on the boat now.

> **Why not visit our duty-free shop before your flight leaves?**

3 You *need to / should* look inside the shop.

> Coach to city centre 15 euros
> Tickets on sale only inside airport

4 You *need to / don't have to* pay before you get on the coach.

> **Passengers only beyond this point – please show boarding pass**

5 If you aren't travelling, you *don't need to / mustn't* go through here.

9 Look at the first diagram and read the example, which describes how to get from Melbourne to Heron Island. Then look at the second diagram and describe how to get from London to Vizzavona in the same way. Then describe a journey of your choice, using as many different means of transport as possible!

EXAMPLE: **Melbourne to Heron Island (Australia)**

✈ ···⟫ Brisbane (change) ✈ ···⟫ Gladstone ···⟫ 🚤 ···⟫ 🚁 ···⟫ Heron Island

*You should fly from Melbourne to Brisbane. You need to change there and take another plane to Gladstone. From Gladstone you needn't take a boat, because there's a helicopter to Heron Island.*

**London to Vizzavona (Corsica)**

✈ ···⟫ Paris (change) ✈ ···⟫ Ajaccio 🚗 ···⟫ 🚕 ···⟫ station ···⟫ 🚌 ···⟫ Vizzavona

# 16.2 A day out

## Speaking

1 Are these sentences about Speaking Part 2 right or wrong? Say why.

1 You must ask another student five questions in this part.
2 You needn't include the information on the card in your answers.
3 You mustn't talk to the examiner during this part.
4 You need to keep to the same words that are on the card.
5 You should try to relax!

2 Student A, turn to page 132 and ask Student B questions about a day trip. Student B turn to page 134 and answer A's questions.

## Listening

3 🎧 You will hear five short conversations. You will hear each conversation twice. For questions 1–5, put a tick under the right answer.

1 Which train is leaving next?

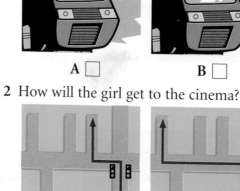

A ☐    B ☐    C ☐

2 How will the girl get to the cinema?

A ☐    B ☐    C ☑

3 Where is Kate's boat now?

A ☐    B ☐    C ☐

4 How will the woman get to work today?

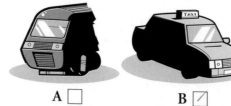

A ☐    B ☑    C ☐

5 Where is the nearest petrol station?

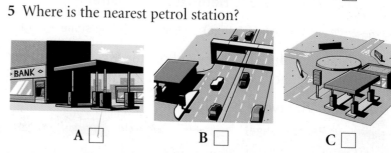

A ☐    B ☐    C ☐

## Pronunciation

4 🎧 We usually say the weak form of the word *of*. Listen again to these examples from the recording.

> *a quarter of an hour ago*
> *because of last night's winds*

🎧 Now listen to these sentences. Does the underlined word sound weak or strong? Write W or S beside each one.

1 We've got <u>some</u> heavy luggage. *W*
2 Why did you go to Greenland, <u>of</u> all places?
3 <u>Some</u> people travel a lot for work.
4 Can I ask you a couple <u>of</u> questions?
5 The journey's by train <u>and</u> coach.
6 Kate's emailed us <u>some</u> directions to the house.
7 My hotel room's very dark, there are no towels, <u>and</u> the TV doesn't work!
8 On the left <u>of</u> the square there's a bank.

## SPELLING SPOT    *i or e?*

KET candidates often confuse the letters *i* and *e*, as in the spelling error *expirience* (for experience).

5 Here are some spelling errors that candidates have made in the KET exam. Correct the sentences. One sentence is correct.

1 Cross the bridge, turn right and the musium is on your left.
2 When you leave the aeroport by car, take the third turning off the roundabout and drive for 5 km.
3 To get to the hospetal, go up Silver Street and turn left at the lights.
4 Go straight past the cinema and turn right at the petrol station.
5 You need to walk along the river, cross the univirsity footbridge and then take the second turning on the right.

## Activity

### How to get there

- Choose a place on the map. Don't tell your partner.
- Give your partner directions to the place. Your partner must say which place it is.

EXAMPLE:

A: *Go over the bridge. Turn right. Take the first turning on the left. This place is on your right. What is it?*

B: *It's the hotel.*

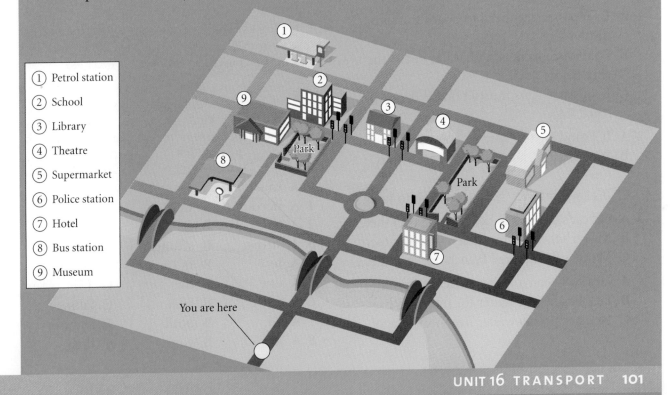

1 Petrol station
2 School
3 Library
4 Theatre
5 Supermarket
6 Police station
7 Hotel
8 Bus station
9 Museum

Park

Park

You are here

## Speaking

1 Write questions for these answers. Then ask your partner the questions. Try to give answers as long as number 8, or longer.

EXAMPLE: *(1) What job would you like to do after you leave school?*

1 I'm not sure, but I'd like to work for an advertising company.
2 It isn't really hot enough today.
3 Sorry, I mustn't be late home this evening.
4 My favourite is an old Italian leather one with deep pockets.
5 I think it's going to rain on Saturday.
6 You don't have to pay anything.
7 I've been to Buenos Aires.
8 The best one I've read this year is a detective story by George Pelecanos.

## Grammar

2 In **1–4** only one sentence is correct. Tick the correct sentence (**A–C**).

1 A Foot passengers need to board the ship until 4.45.
  B Foot passengers don't have to board the ship before 4.45.
  C Foot passengers mustn't board the ship since 4.45.

2 A It's snowing too hard to cycle into town.
  B It's snowing enough hard to cycle into town.
  C It's snowing very hard to cycle into town.

3 A My car's the French new red one over there.
  B My car's the red French new one over there.
  C My car's the new red French one over there.

4 A Jack has been a waiter since five months.
  B Jack has been a waiter for five months.
  C Jack has been a waiter five months ago.

3 Read this text about the weather. Choose the best word (**A, B** or **C**) for each space.

**World weather**

In (**0**) *many* parts of the world, the weather (**1**) ............... change from one minute to the next. The sun (**2**) ............... covered by dark clouds, the wind gets (**3**) ............... than before and it starts to rain. Usually, it doesn't take (**4**) ............... long for the sunny weather to return.

In the Tropics, which are near the Equator, the weather doesn't change for months at (**5**) ............... time. It is very hot and heavy rain (**6**) ............... every day.

At the North and South Poles, it is always cold and there is ice (**7**) ............... year. However, in summer there are many plants near the poles. They grow close to the ground because of the wind and complete (**8**) ............... life cycle in a few weeks.

0 A much      B many      C lots
1 A need      B must      C can
2 A has       B is        C was
3 A strong    B stronger  C strongest
4 A too       B more      C enough
5 A one       B the       C a
6 A fall      B falls     C falling
7 A all       B both      C some
8 A its       B your      C their

# Vocabulary

4 Put the words below into the correct circle. Put the nouns on the left and the verbs on the right. If a word is a noun and a verb, write it in both places. Then make sentences using different nouns and verbs.

EXAMPLE: *The artist Canaletto painted many pictures of Venice.*

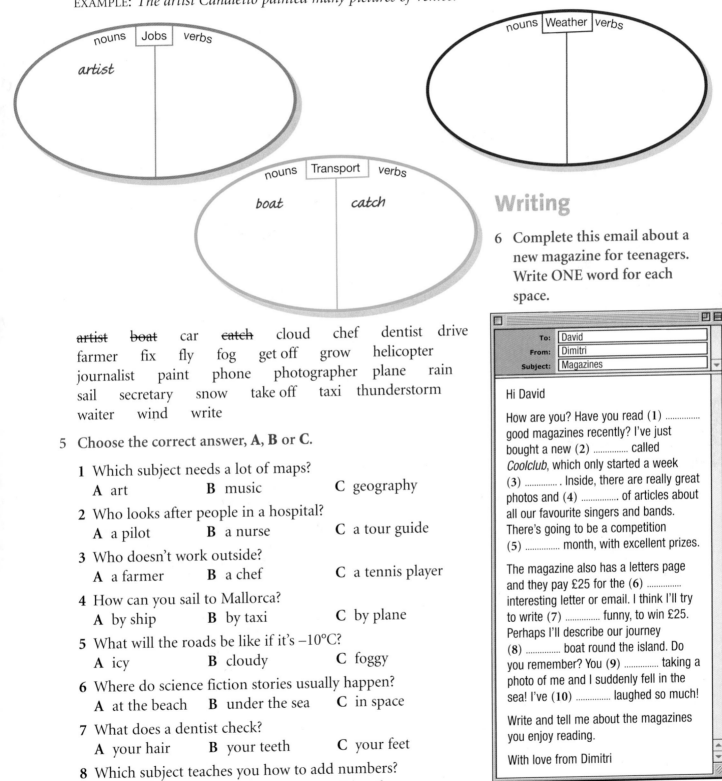

nouns | Jobs | verbs

artist

nouns | Weather | verbs

nouns | Transport | verbs

boat          catch

~~artist~~   ~~boat~~   car   ~~catch~~   cloud   chef   dentist   drive
farmer   fix   fly   fog   get off   grow   helicopter
journalist   paint   phone   photographer   plane   rain
sail   secretary   snow   take off   taxi   thunderstorm
waiter   wind   write

5 Choose the correct answer, **A**, **B** or **C**.

1 Which subject needs a lot of maps?
  **A** art        **B** music        **C** geography

2 Who looks after people in a hospital?
  **A** a pilot        **B** a nurse        **C** a tour guide

3 Who doesn't work outside?
  **A** a farmer        **B** a chef        **C** a tennis player

4 How can you sail to Mallorca?
  **A** by ship        **B** by taxi        **C** by plane

5 What will the roads be like if it's −10°C?
  **A** icy        **B** cloudy        **C** foggy

6 Where do science fiction stories usually happen?
  **A** at the beach        **B** under the sea        **C** in space

7 What does a dentist check?
  **A** your hair        **B** your teeth        **C** your feet

8 Which subject teaches you how to add numbers?
  **A** history        **B** science        **C** maths

# Writing

6 Complete this email about a new magazine for teenagers. Write ONE word for each space.

To: David
From: Dimitri
Subject: Magazines

Hi David

How are you? Have you read (1) .............. good magazines recently? I've just bought a new (2) .............. called *Coolclub*, which only started a week (3) .............. . Inside, there are really great photos and (4) .............. of articles about all our favourite singers and bands. There's going to be a competition (5) .............. month, with excellent prizes.

The magazine also has a letters page and they pay £25 for the (6) .............. interesting letter or email. I think I'll try to write (7) .............. funny, to win £25. Perhaps I'll describe our journey (8) .............. boat round the island. Do you remember? You (9) .............. taking a photo of me and I suddenly fell in the sea! I've (10) .............. laughed so much!

Write and tell me about the magazines you enjoy reading.

With love from Dimitri

## Reading

1  Are you a Technophobe, a Technososo or a Techno Star? Find out by answering the questions in this chart.

## Grammar

### Infinitive of purpose

2  We often use the infinitive (*to* + verb) to say *why* we do things. Find four examples in the quiz and underline them.

**G** ⋯⟫ page 144

**Who are you?**

...TECHNOSOSO?

...TECHNOPHOBE?

...TECHNO STAR?

**Start here**

You have used a computer in the last 24 hours.

NO → Your dad sets the video player for you. ⋯ You think the internet is boring. NO ← YES → You use a computer to talk to people in chat rooms.

YES / NO · Letters are better than emails. NO → YES / NO · You switch on to check your email about once a week. NO ← YES · You have the latest mobile phone.

YES · Writing a text message takes you too long. NO → You use a computer to do your homework. NO · YES · You'd like a robot to help clean your room.

NO

YES → **TECHNOPHOBE** · YES → **TECHNOSOSO** · YES → **TECHNO STAR**

**TECHNOPHOBE**
Oh dear. You don't really like computers or mobile phones, do you? Why don't you give them a try? They might even help your social life.

**TECHNOSOSO**
You aren't afraid of technology, but you haven't forgotten that people are important too. Remember to send your friends a card on their birthday!

**TECHNO STAR**
You're a whizz with gadgets, but could you live without them? Do you have time to see your friends? Do you have any friends?!

3  Complete each sentence with the infinitive form of a verb from the box.

| listen | ~~help~~ | tell |
|--------|----------|------|
| turn on | buy | study |
| call | keep | |

1  You can buy a robot ___to help___ you do your housework.
2  We use a clock _____ the time.
3  You use this switch _____ the computer.
4  Emily needs a mobile phone _____ her friends.
5  A fridge is useful _____ food cool.
6  Paula has a CD player _____ to her favourite music on the train to work.
7  Carlos went to university _____ computer science.
8  My brother is saving all his money _____ the latest computer game.

**Did you know?**
The word 'robot' was first used in 1921 by a man called Karel Capek. 'Robot' means 'a slave' in the Czech language!

**Did you know?**
An Englishman called Charles Babbage built the first 'computer' in 1834. The machine was as big as a bus!

**4** With a partner, talk about why people do these things.

EXAMPLE:
*I think people go to university ...*
*... to learn more about a subject.*
*... to get a good job when they leave.*
*... to have fun.*

1 go to university
2 listen to the radio
3 have parties
4 go to other countries
5 play football
6 use a laptop computer
7 read magazines
8 take photos
9 learn English

**5** Do you play computer games? Why? / Why not?
Which computer games do you like best?
Can people learn anything from playing computer games?

**6** Read the article about the man who made the first Game Boy. Circle the best word (**A, B or C**) for each space.

# Gunpei Yokoi
## (1941 – 1997)

Gunpei Yokoi was born in 1941 and lived in the city (0) .......... Kyoto in Japan. After Gunpei left college he started (1) .......... for a job and in 1965 he went to work at Nintendo. The Nintendo company was started in 1889 (2) .......... make playing cards. Gunpei worked in the games department of (3) .......... company. On his first day there Gunpei had the idea for a new game. Nintendo called it 'Ultrahand'. They sold 1.2 million of the 'Ultrahand' game in its first year. Gunpei (4) .......... began work on video games. He wanted to make cheap machines (5) .......... people could carry in (6) .......... hand. In 1989 Gunpei made the first Game Boy. It is one of the (7) .......... popular games in the world and Nintendo (8) .......... sold millions of these games.

| | | |
|---|---|---|
| 0 (A of) | B by | C over |
| 1 A look | B looked | C looking |
| 2 A for | B to | C at |
| 3 A each | B one | C the |
| 4 A then | B still | C yet |
| 5 A who | B when | C which |
| 6 A his | B its | C their |
| 7 A most | B some | C every |
| 8 A were | B are | C have |

# 17.2 Science is great!

## Listening

1 Have you ever seen a James Bond film? What do you think of the gadgets – the special pens, watches and cameras that James Bond uses?

2 🎧 Listen to Vanessa telling her friend Paul about a visit to see a special James Bond exhibition at the Science Museum in London.

For questions 1–6, tick **A**, **B** or **C**.

0 Vanessa's ticket cost
  A £2.95.
  B £6.50. ✔
  C £8.00.

1 Vanessa went to the museum
  A on foot.
  B on the underground.
  C by bus.

2 Vanessa really liked James Bond's
  A helicopter.
  B car.
  C camera.

3 The museum opens at
  A 9.00.
  B 10.00.
  C 11.30.

4 For lunch Vanessa decided to
  A take a picnic.
  B have a hot meal.
  C get a snack.

5 The exhibition will finish on
  A 23rd April.
  B 24th April.
  C 27th April.

## Pronunciation

3 🎧 Listen again to these sentences from the recording.

There <u>wasn't</u> enough time to see everything.
<u>I'd</u> really like to go.
<u>I'm</u> free next Saturday – <u>that's</u> 23rd April.
The <u>exhibition's</u> on until the 27th.

Write the full version of the underlined contractions.

4 With a partner, underline the words you can contract in the following sentences and then say them aloud. There are two sentences where you can't contract the words.

1 I am going to buy a new calculator.
2 Are you not coming to my house tonight?
3 Who is playing with my Game Boy?
4 I would like a new mobile for my birthday.
5 Who is it?
6 Dan has borrowed my laptop again.
7 They cannot see the exhibition because it has closed.
8 Has she been shopping yet? Yes, she has.

🎧 Listen to check your answers.

# Vocabulary

5 There are many words in English that go together.

Match the verbs below with the nouns. Sometimes there is more than one answer.

| | |
|---|---|
| get | TV |
| make | a noise |
| watch | a job |
| see | a film |
| | friends |

6 Circle the correct word in these questions and then ask your partner the questions.

1 How often do you *make / go* a noise when you have friends to visit?
2 What job do you think you will *get / make* when you leave college?
3 Do you find it easy to *get / make* friends?
4 What do you usually *watch / see* on TV?
5 When do you usually *see / watch* your friends?
6 Have you *seen / watched* any interesting films this week?

## SPELLING SPOT
### Correcting mistakes

7 Read this note from a friend. Correct the spelling mistakes and add commas, capital letters and full stops.

Dear Carl

i want to sell a mobile becose my girlfriend bougth me a new won last weakend it is too yeers old and the prize is about $100 my telefone nummber is 956531

Regards
Phil

## GRAMMAR EXTRA
### The infinitive – with and without *to*

- A number of verbs are followed by *to* + infinitive:

| | |
|---|---|
| decide | *They decided to buy their son a pet.* |
| go | *She went to see the new Bond film.* |
| hope | |
| learn | |
| need | |
| want | |
| would like | |

- These modal verbs are followed by the infinitive **without** *to*:

| | |
|---|---|
| can / could | *We couldn't find the right house.* |
| must | *You mustn't tell anyone.* |
| may / might | |
| shall / should | |
| will / would | |

8 Here are some errors that candidates have made in the KET exam. Correct the sentences.

1 I'd like for see you next weekend.
2 I must to arrive home at 10.00.
3 I would like sell my books.
4 I want buy it.
5 You can to go to a museum there.
6 I have decided study chemistry.
7 She should to visiting London.
8 I hope see you soon.
9 We need doing our homework tonight.
10 We went to London see the London Eye.

## Activity

Write a short description of something you use every day. Read it aloud and let everyone guess what it is.

EXAMPLE:
*It is made of metal and plastic and is quite small. I use it every day. It has numbers on it. I use it to make appointments or find out information.*

# Exam folder 9

## Listening Part 3　Multiple choice

In Part 3 of the Listening paper you must listen to a conversation. There are always two speakers, one male and one female. There are five questions (**11–15**), each with a choice of three answers (**A**, **B** or **C**). These choices can be numbers or words. You must choose the correct answer. There is also an example at the beginning.

### Exam advice

*Before you listen*
- Read through the questions carefully. You have 20 seconds to do this.

*First listening*
- You hear the conversation twice so don't worry if you don't hear all the answers the first time you listen.
- The first time you listen, tick your answers on the question paper. You have time at the end of the test to transfer your answers to your answer sheet.

*Second listening*
- The second time you listen, check to make sure your answers are correct.
- Opposite is an example of the answer sheet for Part 3.

| Part 3 | | | |
|---|---|---|---|
| **11** | A | B | C |
| **12** | A | B | C |
| **13** | A | B | C |
| **14** | A | B | C |
| **15** | A | B | C |

Here are some example questions. Read the question and recording script. All three choices are mentioned in the recording script, but only one choice answers the question.

1　Sam bought the DVD for　**A**　£15.00.
　　　　　　　　　　　　　　**B**　£16.00.
　　　　　　　　　　　　　　**C**　£19.50.

**Judy:** The DVD that you wanted costs £16.00 in the supermarket.
**Sam:** I know, but I was really lucky and got it for £15.00 from the video shop. Last week they were selling it for £19.50, so I'm really pleased.

The answer is **A**.

2　Joe goes to an extra science class every　**A**　Monday.
　　　　　　　　　　　　　　　　　　　　**B**　Tuesday.
　　　　　　　　　　　　　　　　　　　　**C**　Thursday.

**Sue:** There's an extra science class on Tuesdays, isn't there?
**Joe:** That one's for the under 14s. I'm in an older class – that's on Thursdays, and there's one on Mondays as well, but I play football then.

The answer is **C**.

**Part 3**

## Questions 11–15

Listen to Ellie talking to Chris about Lynne, his sister.

For questions **11–15**, tick (✓) **A**, **B** or **C**.
You will hear the conversation twice.

**Example:**

**0**  Lynne arrived home on

A  Monday.  ☐

B  Wednesday.  ☑

C  Saturday.  ☐

---

**11**  At the moment Lynne is working in

A  Hong Kong.  ☐

B  New York.  ☐

C  London.  ☐

**12**  Lynne learnt how to use a computer

A  at home.  ☐

B  at school.  ☐

C  at university.  ☐

**13**  Next year Lynne will get

A  four weeks' holiday.  ☐

B  five weeks' holiday.  ☐

C  six weeks' holiday.  ☐

**14**  Lynne is free

A  in the morning.  ☐

B  at lunchtime.  ☐

C  in the afternoon.  ☐

**15**  Chris has bought Lynne

A  a computer game.  ☐

B  a camera.  ☐

C  a watch.  ☐

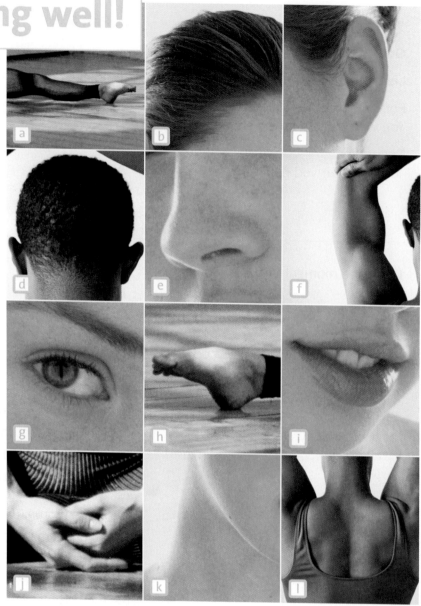

## Vocabulary

1 Put the letters in the right order to spell the name of a part of the body or face. Then match the words with the photos.

EXAMPLE: *head – d*

*The body*
1 e a d h
2 a i r h
3 n e k c
4 m r a
5 n a h d s
6 c k b a
7 e g l
8 f o t o

*The face*
9 r a e
10 h t m o u
11 s e o n
12 y e e

2 Read the descriptions of words to do with health. What is the word for each one? The first letter is already there.

1 A doctor helps people who feel like this.
s *i c k*

2 This person helps people who are ill in hospital.
n _ _ _ _

3 People telephone to ask this to take them to hospital.
a _ _ _ _ _ _ _ _

4 It's important to take this if you want to get better.
m _ _ _ _ _ _ _

5 If this is high, you feel ill.
t _ _ _ _ _ _ _ _ _ _

6 This shop sells things to make people feel better.
c _ _ _ _ _ _

3 Match the sentences **1–10** with the responses **A–J**. (Some can be used more than once.)

EXAMPLE: *1 H*

1 I'm very tired.
2 I've got a terrible headache.
3 I've got a cold.
4 I'm too fat.
5 How do you feel today?
6 My foot hurts.
7 I've cut my hand.
8 I've broken my arm.
9 I've got a sore throat.
10 I've got stomach ache.

A You probably need an X-ray.
B Why don't you go on a diet?
C Terrible. I think I'll stay in bed.
D Go and lie down.
E You need a hot lemon drink.
F Don't go running today.
G You need a plaster.
H Try going to bed earlier.
I Try not to talk.
J You should take an aspirin.

4   Look at the pictures below. Tell your partner what the problem is. Your partner will give you some advice.

Begin:   *I've …*
Answer:  *You should … / You need … / Why don't you …?*

## Listening

5   🎧 You will hear some information about which chemists are open in the local area.

Listen and complete questions 1–5.

**Information**

Date:   15th–21st December

*Bridges* in Sandford

*Bridges'* opening hours (Mon–Fri):
          (1) 8.45 am – ..................

Nearest chemist when *Bridges* is closed

Name of shop:   (2) ................................................
Address:          (3) ............ The High Street, Dursley.
Opposite:         (4) ................................................
Telephone no:   (5) ................................................

**GRAMMAR EXTRA**

**Word order of time phrases**

• In the recording in exercise 5 the man said:
  *Ring this number if you need to talk to the chemist at night.*
• The time phrase (*at night*) is used after the object (*the chemist*).
• We usually use a time phrase either at the beginning of a sentence/clause or at the end.
  **Last Saturday** *we went running after school.*
  *We went running after school* **last Saturday**.

6   Here are some errors that candidates have made in the KET exam. Correct the sentences.

1   I was last night at a big party.
2   I'll come on Saturday shopping.
3   We have been every day to the beach.
4   I went after work to the chemist.
5   They at night usually sleep well.
6   I bought today some new trainers.

## Pronunciation

When we speak we link together the consonant sound at the end of a word and the vowel sound at the beginning of the next word.

7   🎧 Listen and mark the linking in these sentences.

EXAMPLE:   *He's got a broken arm.*
            *We're here to make an appointment.*

1   Can you call an ambulance?
2   Fruit and vegetables are very good for you.
3   You should do some exercise every day.
4   Watching TV all weekend is not good for you.
5   Make sure you get enough sleep every night.

1 Some people say that if you sleep about six to seven hours a night, you will have a long and happy life. How many hours a night do you sleep?

## Reading

2 Read the article quickly to find out who is the oldest person mentioned.

Now read it again more slowly. Are sentences 1–8 'Right' (**A**) or 'Wrong' (**B**)? If there is not enough information to answer 'Right' (**A**) or 'Wrong' (**B**), choose 'Doesn't say' (**C**).

1 Doctors now think that Shirali Muslimov was probably younger than he thought he was.
   **A** Right      **B** Wrong      **C** Doesn't say

2 Kamato Hongo lived a long life because she only ate vegetables.
   **A** Right      **B** Wrong      **C** Doesn't say

3 Joan Riudavets Moll sleeps less now than he did when he was younger.
   **A** Right      **B** Wrong      **C** Doesn't say

4 Joan's first job was working in a hospital.
   **A** Right      **B** Wrong      **C** Doesn't say

5 Joan was married three times.
   **A** Right      **B** Wrong      **C** Doesn't say

6 Joan spends most of his time in his house.
   **A** Right      **B** Wrong      **C** Doesn't say

7 Joan remembers life without electricity.
   **A** Right      **B** Wrong      **C** Doesn't say

8 Joan enjoyed playing football.
   **A** Right      **B** Wrong      **C** Doesn't say

Some of the oldest people in the world are said to live in Azerbaijan. The most famous of all was Shirali Muslimov, who died on 2 September 1973 at the age of 168. Today, doctors do not think this is possible, but he was a very old man – probably nearer 120 than 160!

Another person who was once the oldest person in the world was Kamato Hongo. She was born in 1887, in Japan, and died in 2003 at the age of 116. Kamato usually slept for two full days at a time and then was awake for two full days. She said to live a long life you mustn't 'think too much', and her favourite things were sugar, steak and green tea.

Joan Riudavets Moll was born on 15 December 1889, on the Balearic Island of Menorca. He still lives there, spending up to 14 hours a day asleep. Riudavets really wanted to be a doctor but he became a shoemaker, working at home in the family business. He has three daughters in all, with five grandsons and six great-grandchildren. He rarely leaves his home. He thinks planes and electricity are the most important changes he has seen in his life. During his life he has played a lot of football – his favourite game – and still enjoys singing and playing the guitar. What does Joan Riudavets Moll say about living a long life? 'If you eat a little but often, you will live a long life.'

# Grammar

## First conditional

- Find the sentence in the text which begins with *If ...*

  *If* ......................................................................................................... .

- Which tenses are used?

  *If +* ......................................................................................................... .

- We use this structure to express a possible condition.

**3** Match the sentences below.

| | |
|---|---|
| **1** If I get up 7.00 o'clock, | **A** I'll get a good job. |
| **2** If I go swimming every day, | **B** I'll travel round the world. |
| **3** If I work hard at school, | **C** I'll sleep better at night. |
| **4** If I save my money, | **D** I'll get fit. |
| **5** If I win the lottery, | **E** I won't be late for school. |
| **6** If I drink less coffee, | **F** I'll buy a TV for my bedroom. |

- When the sentence begins with *if*, we often use a comma. We can also use *if* in the middle of a sentence without a comma.

**G** ⋯⋯⋗ **page 145**

**4** We all need enough sleep at night. What other things will make you healthier? Talk to your partner about the things below and add two more ideas of your own.

| | |
|---|---|
| **1** eating hamburgers | **4** too much stress |
| **2** riding a motorbike | **5** having a holiday |
| **3** working long hours | **6** drinking lots of water |

......................................................................................................

......................................................................................................

**5** You are going on a camping holiday in the mountains with a friend. What problems do you think you may have?

EXAMPLE: A: *What will you do if you have an accident?*
B: *I'll use my mobile phone to ring someone.*

**6** Complete the sentences.

If I work harder, I will ...     If I don't ...
If I get up ...     If ...

**7** Write a note to a friend about what you are going to do to become healthier. Say:

- why you want to get fit
- what you are going to do
- when or how often you are going to do it.

Write 25–35 words.

## SPELLING SPOT

### Words which don't double their last letter

The last letter isn't doubled if a word ends in

- two consonants:

  *help   helped   helping*

- two vowels and a consonant:

  *need   needed   needing*

**8** Are these words correct? Put a tick or a cross beside each one.

1 cheaper
2 fastter
3 getting
4 stoping
5 waiting
6 running
7 thiner
8 swiming

## Activity

### Sleep and dreams

- Every night we dream at least three times. Ask four of your classmates about their sleeping habits.

**1** Do you sleep on your back, your side or your front?

**2** Do you remember your dreams?

**3** Do you ever have bad dreams?

**4** What do you do if you wake up in the night?

**5** What do you do if you have problems getting to sleep?

- Report back to the class.

# Exam folder 10

## Reading Part 4    Multiple choice

In Part 4 of the Reading and Writing paper you must read one long article or three short articles. There are seven questions (**21–27**) and an example at the beginning. Each question has a choice of three answers (**A**, **B** or **C**). You must choose the correct answer.

### Exam advice

- Read the article(s) all the way through before you the read the questions.
- Don't worry if there is a word you don't understand.
- Read each question very carefully. The questions are in the order in which you will find the answers in the article(s).
- Underline the place in the article(s) where you find the answer.
- Mark your answer on your answer sheet. Opposite is an example of the answer sheet for Part 4.

| Part 4 | | | |
|--------|---|---|---|
| 21 | A | B | C |
| 22 | A | B | C |
| 23 | A | B | C |
| 24 | A | B | C |
| 25 | A | B | C |
| 26 | A | B | C |
| 27 | A | B | C |

## Part 4

**Questions 21–27**

Read the article about a famous Australian man, called John Flynn.

For questions **21–27**, mark **A**, **B** or **C** on your answer sheet.

# The Flying Doctor

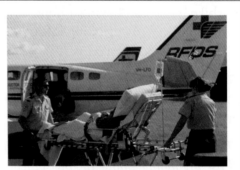

John Flynn was born in Australia in 1880. His father was a schoolteacher. John studied hard and in 1911 he left the city of Melbourne and went to work in South Australia for the Presbyterian Church. The church wanted to help the sheep farmers who lived in the outback – the countryside area many kilometres from towns and cities. They built a number of small hospitals and found nurses to work in them. But at that time there were only two doctors in all of South Australia.

One story Flynn often told was of Jimmy Darcy. One day Jimmy had an accident on his farm so friends took him to see F.W. Tuckett, who worked at the post office at Halls Creek. It was a journey of 22 km. Tuckett was the only person in the area who knew anything about medicine. He tried to help but Jimmy was too ill. Tuckett finally talked by radio to a doctor in Perth, a city 1500 km away. The doctor took ten days to arrive. He travelled by car, by horse and on foot and when he arrived, he found that Jimmy was already dead.

Flynn saw that planes could really help people in the outback. He wrote about his idea for a 'Flying Doctor' in 1917 but it wasn't until 1928 that one actually took off. By the 1930s there was a Flying Doctor plane in every part of Australia.

**Example:**

**0** John Flynn's job was    **A** teaching at a school.

                        **B** helping with sheep farming.

                        **C** working for the church.     *Answer:*   0   A B C

---

**21** Flynn worked in

                        **A** a city.

                        **B** the countryside.

                        **C** a small town.

**22** What was the problem in South Australia?

                        **A** The nurses weren't very good.

                        **B** There were no hospitals.

                        **C** There weren't enough doctors.

**23** What does Flynn tell us about Jimmy?

                        **A** He lived at Halls Creek.

                        **B** He was a farmer.

                        **C** He was often ill.

**24** Why did Jimmy and his friends go to see F.W. Tuckett?

                        **A** He helped sick people.

                        **B** He worked at a post office.

                        **C** He was a doctor.

**25** What did F.W. Tuckett decide to do?

                        **A** to give Jimmy some medicine

                        **B** to go with Jimmy to the city

                        **C** to use a radio to get help for Jimmy

**26** What do we know about the doctor from Perth?

                        **A** He travelled too slowly to save Jimmy.

                        **B** He had problems with his car.

                        **C** He didn't know the way to Halls Creek.

**27** The first Flying Doctor plane flew in

                        **A** 1917.

                        **B** 1928.

                        **C** 1930.

## Vocabulary

1 Find seventeen words to do with communicating in the word square (look → and ↓). Use the pictures to help you. The first one has been done for you.

| a | l | i | o | r | o | m | a | y | i |
|---|---|---|---|---|---|---|---|---|---|
| w | e | n | v | e | l | o | p | e | n |
| r | t | f | o | c | c | b | o | s | t |
| i | t | a | f | e | a | i | s | r | e |
| t | e | x | t | i | l | l | t | i | r |
| e | r | n | e | v | l | e | c | n | n |
| n | w | e | m | e | s | s | a | g | e |
| o | c | h | a | t | o | m | r | i | t |
| t | o | r | i | s | e | n | d | a | l |
| e | t | e | l | e | p | h | o | n | e |

2 Which ways of communicating are best in these situations? Decide on your answers, then talk to another student about them, using words from the word square.

1 Your friend in Australia has a birthday in a couple of days, so it's too late to post anything.
2 You've heard that your cousin in another town is getting married.
3 You can't meet your friends tonight and want to say sorry.
4 You want to tell your family where you'll be this evening but no one is at home.
5 You're on holiday and want to show your brother what the place is like.
6 A friend who lives near you has just had some bad news.

## Listening

3 🎧 Listen to Paul talking about how he has communicated some good news. Which way of communicating has he used for each person?

For questions 1–5, write a letter (A–H) next to each person.

EXAMPLE: **0** Ruth    | B |

| **People** | | **Ways of communicating** |
|---|---|---|
| 1 Mario | ☐ | **A** email |
| 2 Anna | ☐ | **B** fax |
| 3 Jack | ☐ | **C** letter |
| 4 Tessa | ☐ | **D** mobile phone call |
| 5 Paul's professor | ☐ | **E** note |
| | | **F** phone message |
| | | **G** postcard |
| | | **H** text |

## Pronunciation

4 🎧 Listen again to the parts of the recording below. For the words broken into syllables, put a star to mark which syllable is stressed.

1 Con|gra|tu|la*|tions on the new job!
2 I didn't have your e|mail address.
3 I left a mess|age on her an|swer|phone.
4 Yes, in Ar|gen|ti|na.
5 Re|mem|ber to phone your pro|fess|or and tell him.
6 The num|ber at his u|ni|ver|si|ty has changed.
7 I bought one of that Mo|rocc|an car|pet we saw at the mu|se|um.

## Grammar   Prepositions of place

In the recording, you heard several phrases with prepositions, for example, *I got your fax* **at work** *this morning.*

5 Complete each phrase with a preposition from the box and add another similar phrase of your own.

| at | in | on |
|----|----|----|

1 _at_ home              _at work_ ............................
2 .......... the floor    ............................
3 .......... Argentina    ............................
4 .......... New Street   ............................
5 .......... 25 Broad Street ............................
6 .......... Madrid       ............................
7 .......... the bus stop ............................

6 Here are some errors that candidates have made with prepositions in the KET exam. Correct the sentences. One sentence is correct.

1 You can call me at my cell phone: 22 59 67 81.
2 I'll meet you on the supermarket in West Street.
3 I'm in holiday now in Istanbul.
4 You can stay on my house.
5 The hotel is at the centre of the town.
6 We live on a new house in Magka.
7 On the walls there are some posters.
8 If you are interested, find me at room 12.

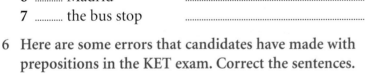 page 145

## 7 Complete this letter. Write ONE word for each space.

Dear Margareta

How are you? With email, I don't write too **(1)** .............. letters now, but I'm sending you one **(2)** .............. I know you like to receive them. I've bought **(3)** .............. beautiful stamps to put **(4)** .............. the envelope, too. **(5)** .............. my country, the post office often sells stamps showing different birds, like **(6)** .............. . I think they're great! **(7)** .............. one is your favourite?

If you get a computer at home soon, **(8)** .............. you have an email address? Please let **(9)** .............. know about that.

My mum and dad and **(10)** .............. else in the family send you their best wishes.

Love,

Agnes

### SPELLING SPOT    /iː/

- The sound /iː/ is spelled in different ways in English.

| beginning | middle | end |
|-----------|--------|-----|
| <u>e</u>mail | b<u>ee</u>n | s<u>ee</u> |
| <u>ea</u>sy | m<u>ea</u>n | t<u>ea</u> |
|  | th<u>e</u>se | w<u>e</u> |
|  | pol<u>i</u>ce |  |
|  | bel<u>ie</u>ve |  |
|  | c<u>ei</u>ling |  |

8 Fill in the missing vowels.

1 Have you rec_ _ved an email from Jan yet?
2 Here's a fr_ _ pen for you. They cost 6 euros _ _ch in the shops!
3 Can I sp_ _k to Mrs Lee?
4 What animals are in that f_ _ld over there?
5 I'm going to be away all next w_ _k.
6 I'd like a k_lo of apples.

# 19.2 Different languages

1 Do you speak another language or dialect at home or with friends? Do your grandparents?

## Reading

2 Are there more or fewer dialects in your country today than 20 years ago? Why?

3 Read this article about the Cornish language. Choose the best word for each space, **A**, **B** or **C**.

# The history of Cornish

**A**round 4000 years (**0**) ............, the group of languages now called the Celtic languages started to develop. (**1**) ............ languages then became two different groups. Cornish, Welsh and Breton – the language spoken (**2**) ............ north-west France – are one group, and Irish and Scots Gaelic are part of the (**3**) ............ .

Cornish grew like a modern European language (**4**) ............ the 17th century, when English became (**5**) ............ important in Cornwall than earlier. English (**6**) ............ used to buy and sell things and because of that, Cornish people began to think badly of (**7**) ............ language and lots saw Cornish only as the language of poor people.

By the end of the 19th century, Cornish was no longer spoken. But a man called Henry Jenner studied the language and (**8**) ............ it back to life. Now, you can even learn Cornish on the internet!

| | | |
|---|---|---|
| **0** A ago | B before | C since |
| **1** A This | B Them | C These |
| **2** A on | B in | C at |
| **3** A another | B others | C other |
| **4** A to | B until | C for |
| **5** A more | B much | C many |
| **6** A is | B has | C was |
| **7** A its | B their | C her |
| **8** A bring | B bringing | C brought |

# Grammar  Prepositions of time

4  Check your understanding by filling in the missing prepositions of time: *at, in, on.*

- We use ............... with:

  | | |
  |---|---|
  | years | ............... 1953 |
  | centuries | ............... the 20th century |
  | seasons | ............... (the) summer |
  | months | ............... November |
  | parts of the day | ............... the afternoon |

- We use ............... with:

  | | |
  |---|---|
  | days of the week | ............... Saturday |
  | special days | ............... New Year's Day |
  | dates | ............... 1 March 2004 |

- We use ............... with:

  | | |
  |---|---|
  | times | ............... ten o'clock / 10.00 |
  | meals | ............... breakfast |
  | festivals / | ............... Easter |
  | periods of time | ............... the weekend |

G ⋯⟩ page 146

5  Lara studies German and Russian. Ask and answer questions to complete her timetable, using prepositions of time. Student B should turn to page 133 now.

Student A's questions

- Which day ... German/Russian Conversation?
- What time?
- When ... free?

Do the same for these classes in each language:

| | |
|---|---|
| Conversation | Grammar |
| Reading | Writing |
| Listening | |

EXAMPLE:
A: *Which day does she have German conversation?*
B: *On Monday.*
A: *What time?*
B: *At three o'clock.*

6  How many languages do you know the names of? Remember that sometimes the word used for the language is the same word as the nationality. Complete the table.

| country | nationality | language(s) spoken |
|---|---|---|
| Argentina | Argentinian | |
| Brazil | Brazilian | |
| Chile | Chilean | |
| France | French | |
| Greece | Greek | |
| Italy | Italian | |
| Mexico | Mexican | |
| Morocco | Moroccan | |
| Switzerland | Swiss | |

## Activity

**What do they speak in ...?**

- Get into two teams (and close your books!). Your teacher will give each of you a number.
- When your number is called, say the name of a country. The person with the same number on the opposite team must tell you any one language which is spoken in that country.

  EXAMPLE:  Team A person: *Belgium*
  Team B person: *Flemish*

- Score one point for your team for every language you name correctly.

| | Monday | Tuesday | Wednesday | Thursday | Friday |
|---|---|---|---|---|---|
| 9.00 | | | | | |
| 10.00 | | | | | |
| 11.00 | | | | | |
| 12.00 | | | | | |
| 1.00 | | | LUNCH | | |
| 2.00 | | | | | |
| 3.00 | German Conversation | | | | |

# Writing folder 5

## Writing Part 9  Short message

In Part 9 (Question **56**) of the Reading and Writing paper, you must write about three different things, using between 25 and 35 words. Sometimes, as in Writing folder 3 (see page 72), you will have to reply to a message from a friend. Sometimes there will just be instructions about what you have to write.

1  Look at these KET answers and decide what three things the candidates were asked to write about. Choose from A–E in the box below.

**1**
> Dear Pat
> I'll be free at 10 a.m. We can meet us to Paul's caffe. I'd like to buy a skirt. See you on Saturday.
> Love Anya

**2**
> Dear Pat: I will go for two hours. I will meet with John and I will want buy a red bicycle. Your friend

**3**
> Dear Pat I think it is a great idea to go shopping together. We could meet in the bus stop at 12 o'clock in the morning. I'd like to buy some pens. See you soon. Claudia

**4**
> Yes, I coming with you to shopping on Saturday. I'll probably be free at the lunch. We'll meet us to the shopping centre in town. I want to buy me two trousers and a top. Perhaps, I want to buy also a robe. And you, what do you want to buy?
> From your best friend
> Sylvie

> **A** when you can meet your friend Pat on Saturday
> **B** who you will invite to go shopping with you on Saturday
> **C** where you suggest meeting your friend Pat on Saturday
> **D** what you would like to buy on Saturday
> **E** how you will get to the shopping centre on Saturday

2  Decide which answer is the best and which is the worst. Explain why.

3  Correct any wrong prepositions in the answers and underline other errors.

4  Rewrite answer 4, correcting the errors. Write between 25 and 35 words.

## Exam advice

- Read the question carefully and underline the three things you have to write about.
- Make some quick notes.
- Include an opening formula like *Dear* ... or *Hi* ... with the name.
- Write a rough answer on the question paper first.
- Make sure you write enough words (around 35 is best).
- Use informal English because you are writing to a friend.
- Remember to sign the message with your first name at the end.
- Try to include different nouns and adjectives to show your language range.
- Check grammar, spelling, punctuation and use of capital letters.
- Write your final answer on your answer sheet. Below is an example of the answer sheet for Part 9.

**Part 9 (Question 56): Write your answer below.**

---

## Part 9

### Question 56

You are going to meet your friend Jan at the cinema tomorrow. Write an email to Jan.

Say:

- **when** you will meet at the cinema
- **which film** you want to see
- **why** Jan would enjoy this film.

Write **25–35** words.
Write your email on the answer sheet.

# 20.1 Famous people

1 Who are these people? Why are they famous? Will they still be famous in five years' time? Why? / Why not?

2 Are you interested in famous people? Who are you a fan of? How do you find out about them?

3 With a partner, answer the questions below by choosing **A, B** or **C**.

**A** David Beckham
**B** Kelly Osbourne
**C** Arnold Schwarzenegger

1 Who was born in 1975?
2 Who was born in a small village in Austria?
3 Who became famous because of a television programme on MTV?
4 Who won competitions for having a strong body?
5 Who bought a $75,000 watch but never wears it?

## Grammar
### Review of tenses

4 Circle the correct tense.

1 I think David Beckham *will not play* / *does not play* again for Manchester United.
2 In October 2003, Arnold Schwarzenegger *has become* / *became* Governor of California.
3 Kelly Osbourne *has given* / *gave* many concerts in different countries.
4 During Real Madrid's tour of China in July 2003, large numbers of fans *welcomed* / *were welcoming* David Beckham everywhere.
5 Arnold Schwarzenegger hurt his back once during filming, when he fell off a rock he *was climbing* / *climbed*.
6 Kelly Osbourne *fights* / *is fighting* with her younger brother Jack quite a lot.

**G** ⋯⟶ page 146

5 Who are the most famous man and woman in your country today? Write sentences about them, saying:

– when and where they were born
– what has happened in their lives
– how they became famous
– what they are doing at the moment
– what their lives will be like in five years' time.

6 Tick any tenses you have used in your sentences in exercise 5.

| | |
|---|---|
| present simple | ☐ |
| present continuous | ☐ |
| past simple | ☐ |
| past continuous | ☐ |
| present perfect | ☐ |
| future with *will* | ☐ |

# Reading

7 Read the article about a David Beckham fan called Jenna. Then answer the questions by choosing **A, B** or **C**.

**IN** 2003, 14-year-old Jenna spoke to a journalist of ours about moving to Spain.

'I've only been a Beckham fan for a couple of years but my dad always loved seeing him play at Manchester United. It took him ten hours to get there by car from Cornwall! Mum also follows Becks now. When she and I heard he was leaving to play in Spain, I said, 'Let's move to Spain!' Dad agreed to come but my older brother decided to stay in England. He's still living in our house there.

At first we didn't know if Becks would play for Barcelona or Madrid, so my parents bought a place in Alicante. It's only about three hours away from both cities. Our new home has three bedrooms and two bathrooms on one floor, and there's a flat with another two bedrooms and bathrooms under that. There's a pool, too.

My friends in England will come and visit for my birthday in February. They think I'm a bit mad but they're pleased for me too. I email them all the time. It's great to live in another country and learn a new language, but I'm finding Spanish quite difficult. I learned French in England and I keep mixing the two. It'll be easier when I start at my new school.

Becks is playing really well in Spain, which keeps my dad happy! What I love most about him is that he's a big family man. Being famous hasn't changed him. I'm having a great time in Spain and I'd really like to meet Becks one day.'

Haven't I seen her before?

1 During the years that David Beckham played for Manchester United,
   A Jenna always liked him.
   B Jenna's mother followed his team.
   C Jenna's father drove to his matches.

2 Who had the idea of moving to Spain?
   A Jenna
   B Jenna's father
   C Jenna's brother

3 Jenna's family bought the house in Alicante
   A after they sold their house in Cornwall.
   B before Beckham signed for Real Madrid.
   C when Jenna's father was working in Barcelona.

4 The house in Alicante has
   A an apartment downstairs.
   B a bathroom in every bedroom.
   C two swimming pools.

5 Jenna's friends in England
   A never receive emails from her.
   B haven't visited her yet.
   C aren't happy about her move.

6 Jenna is having problems learning Spanish because
   A her lessons at school are too hard.
   B everyone speaks English to her.
   C she can't stop using French words.

7 Jenna thinks the best thing about Beckham is how
   A he plays football.
   B he loves his children.
   C he enjoys being famous.

8 Find examples in the article of the tenses listed in exercise 6.

# 20.2 Lucky people

## Pronunciation

4 🎧 Listen again to how Ruth asks these questions. Underline the word she stresses most in each one.

1 What have I won?
2 When do we have to use them by?
3 Will you send me the tickets?
4 Where are you?
5 When shall I come?
6 What time?

## Speaking

5 Now it's your turn to ask questions. Student A should turn to page 133. Student B should turn to page 134.

1 Do you believe that some people have better luck than others? Why? / Why not?

2 You have won a competition. Your prize is to visit the city of your choice with one other person. Who will you take? Where will you go? Why?

## Listening

3 🎧 You will hear a girl called Ruth phoning a radio station about a prize she has won. Listen and complete questions 1–5.

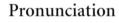

ST★R RADIO
**COMPETITION**

Prize: trip to                 *Venice*
Type of transport:        **(1)** ...........................
Latest date to travel:   **(2)** ........................... *April*
Radio station's address: **(3)** *47* ........................... *Road*
Day to visit the office:  **(4)** ...........................
Time to arrive:            **(5)** ...........................

# Vocabulary

6 Read the descriptions of some adjectives about people. What is the word for each one? What is the adjective in the yellow box? Explain what it means.

1 You can describe your best friend as this.  s _ _ _ _ _ _
2 Those who help other people are said to be this.  k _ _ _
3 This word describes someone who is not married.  s _ _ _ _ _
4 Anyone who gets top marks at school is this.  c _ _ _ _ _
5 If you are laughing, this is how you will feel.  h _ _ _ _

# Reading

7 Read the sentences about a teenage millionaire. Choose the best word (A, B or C) for each space.

1 Jason Richards has always .............................. to play computer games.
   A enjoyed      B loved        C invited

2 When he was 15, he had a good .............................. for a new game.
   A example      B study        C idea

3 Jason went to several computer .............................. to talk about his game.
   A stations     B companies    C houses

4 Nobody was .............................. in selling Jason's game.
   A interested   B ready        C pleased

5 Jason .............................. to sell his game himself on the internet.
   A thought      B agreed       C decided

6 In less than a year, Jason .............................. over £1,000,000 in sales.
   A earned       B paid         C spent

## SPELLING SP T                                                    ck or k?

- If the vowel before the /k/ sound is short, the spelling is 'ck': *Beckham   luck*

- With a short double vowel before the /k/ sound, there is no 'c': *cook*

- If the vowel sound is long, there is no 'c': *break   like*

- If a vowel is followed by a consonant, there is no 'c': *milk   bank*

8 Sort the letters in these words and use them in the sentences below.

o o b   k j   c i k   k o   l u   y   c t i
g i   a   c   n e       s   k
k n   t e   h c   c c   k c   t e

1 There's a TV programme about jazz at nine o'.............................. .
2 Can I borrow your .............................. to wear to the theatre?
3 Let's phone the .............................. office now and get some .............................. for the festival.
4 How .............................. are you? You've won first prize again!
5 This .............................. and rice dish is wonderful. Is there any more?

## Activity

**Millionaire quiz**

Answer your teacher's questions and win money for your team!

## Speaking

1 Ask and answer these questions with a partner.

1 Why do people go on diets?
2 What will you do if you pass KET?
3 Where is the city of Salamanca?
4 Which film actors or directors have won an Oscar?
5 Who do you think you will see next weekend?
6 How much fruit do you eat in a week?
7 When is your birthday?
8 What time will today's lesson finish?

## Grammar

2 Match a phrase from **A** with a phrase from **B** and make conditional sentences.

EXAMPLE: *If I buy a new mobile, I'll be able to send photos.*

| A | B |
|---|---|
| 1 buy a new mobile | invite all my friends |
| 2 get a Saturday job | visit some new websites |
| 3 become famous | go out clubbing |
| 4 eat more healthily | be able to send photos |
| 5 have a party | earn some money |
| 6 do all my homework | get a cup of coffee |
| 7 go on the internet | feel better |
| 8 take a break soon | build a house with a pool |

3 Correct any wrong prepositions in this text about the island of Martinique.

Martinique is the largest island on the area of the Eastern Caribbean. Over 300,000 people live at the island – many on the capital city, Fort-de-France. People speak French and it is taught on schools.

The mountains on Martinique are old volcanos. The highest one is Mount Pelée, which is 1,397 metres high. At 1902, Mount Pelée erupted and about 30,000 people were killed.

The weather at Martinique is warm and quite wet – perfect for the farmers to grow bananas in their land. Bananas from Martinique are sent all over the world, so look at the bananas on your fruit bowl. If they are from Martinique, they will have a blue sticker in them.

## Vocabulary

4 Decide which word is the odd one out.

1 laptop   internet   robot   chatroom
2 ear   mouth   eye   back
3 email   letter   postcard   envelope
4 German   Japanese   Italian   Spanish
5 prize   exam   competition   test
6 lucky   happy   special   ready

5 Read the sentences about recording a TV programme. Choose the best word (**A**, **B** or **C**) for each space.

1 My sister ................ me to video a programme about tigers for her.
 **A** invited   **B** asked   **C** decided

2 I wanted to ................ something else at the same time.
 **A** watch   **B** look   **C** take

3 Because of this, I ................ the video to record her programme.
 **A** put   **B** cut   **C** set

4 By mistake, I chose the ................ TV channel.
 **A** bad   **B** wrong   **C** open

5 My sister was very angry when she ................ a gardening programme on the tape and no tigers!
 **A** found   **B** turned   **C** kept

## Writing

6 Read questions **A** and **B** and decide which sentences (**1–6** below) go with each question. Then put each set of sentences in order, adding a few more words to make a 35-word email that answers each question.

**A**

> You saw someone famous when you were in your capital city last week.
>
> Write an email to your friend, saying:
> - which famous person you saw
> - where you were at the time
> - how you felt.

**B**

> You would like to invite your friend to a party.
>
> Write an email to your friend, saying:
> - when you are going to have the party
> - who else you have invited
> - what you would like your friend to bring.

1 Heidi and Lorna can come as well. *A*
2 It was amazing and I couldn't believe it!
3 Could I borrow your CD player?
4 It'll be on Saturday 15th November, starting at 8.30pm.
5 Tom Cruise walked by just in front of me.
6 I was looking at a painting in an art gallery.

# Extra material

## 1.2 Activity

### Questionnaire

| | |
|---|---|
| Name | |
| Age | |
| Address | |
| Favourite music | |
| Favourite place(s) | |
| What makes you laugh? | |

## 6.2 Activity

### Group A

**How often do you watch TV?**

every night      only at weekends      not often

**What is your favourite free time activity at home?**

playing CDs                reading books

playing chess              seeing friends

playing computer games     something else

......................................

**What is your least favourite free time activity at home?**

......................................

**Add some more questions here:**

......................................
......................................
......................................
......................................
......................................

### Group B

**What is your favourite free time physical activity?**

football                 swimming

tennis                   skateboarding

running                  something else

.................................

**How often do you do a physical activity?**

every day           three times a week

once a week         less than once a week

**What is your least favourite free time physical activity?**

.................................................

**Add some more questions here:**

.................................................
.................................................
.................................................
.................................................

## 9.2 Activity

# ARE YOU A WORLD TRAVELLER?

**1 How often do you go on holiday?**

A hardly ever
B once a year
C twice a year or more

**2 How many countries have you visited?**

A two
B none
C six or more

**3 You win the lottery – where will you go?**

A to Disney World for a month
B to an expensive hotel in my country
C on a trip round the world

**4 What type of holiday do you like?**

A staying at home doing nothing
B activity holidays such as sailing
C lying on a far away beach and dancing all night

**5 Your hotel room isn't very nice. Do you**

A complain to the manager?
B not worry about it?
C not notice?

**6 What do you buy on holiday?**

A presents for all your friends
B one or two souvenirs
C some sweets for yourself

**7 Do you send postcards?**

A no – never
B yes – to everyone I know
C yes – to a few friends

**8 Who do you like to go on holiday with?**

A no one – I prefer to be alone
B my best friend
C my family

Now turn to page 130 to find your score.

## 9.2 Activity

ARE YOU A WORLD TRAVELLER?

**Key**

| | A | | B | | C | |
|---|---|---|---|---|---|---|
| 1 | A | 1 | B | 2 | C | 3 |
| 2 | A | 2 | B | 1 | C | 3 |
| 3 | A | 2 | B | 1 | C | 3 |
| 4 | A | 1 | B | 2 | C | 3 |
| 5 | A | 3 | B | 2 | C | 1 |
| 6 | A | 3 | B | 2 | C | 1 |
| 7 | A | 1 | B | 3 | C | 2 |
| 8 | A | 3 | B | 2 | C | 1 |

**World Traveller 21–24 points**
You really like holidays and enjoy everything about them: buying presents, seeing friends and having fun. But remember, you can have fun at home too!

**Happy Tourist 12–20 points**
You like to go to new places. You enjoy quiet holidays with a few friends and you prefer not to spend too much money.

**Stay-at-Home 8–11 points**
You quite like going away, but you prefer to be with people you know. You are also happy at home. You believe holidays should be relaxing.

# Exam folder 5

Candidate B questions

### Holiday Centre

★ where?

★ what / do?

★ price / adult?

★ open / all year?

★ place / eat?

## 11.1  Exercise 10

# College Sports Day

to be held on the
College Sports Field on
Saturday 12 June (10.00–3.30)

Football, volleyball and
running for everyone.

Win one of
50 T-shirts!

Don't forget your shorts and trainers!

# Exam folder 5

Candidate A questions

### Cinema

- what / see?
- cinema / open?
- eat?
- what / address?
- student ticket / £?

## 16.2 Exercise 2

Student A questions

DAY TRIP FOR STUDENTS
- where?
- when?
- cost?
- transport?
- things to do?

## 19.2 Exercise 5

| | Monday | Tuesday | Wednesday | Thursday | Friday |
|---|---|---|---|---|---|
| 9.00 | German Grammar | | Russian Reading | | Russian Grammar |
| 10.00 | | German Writing | | | Russian Writing |
| 11.00 | | | Russian Conversation | | |
| 12.00 | Russian Listening | | | German Reading | |
| 1.00 | LUNCH | | | | |
| 2.00 | | | German Listening | | |
| 3.00 | German Conversation | | | | |

## 20.2 Exercise 5

### Student A questions

Ask Student B about his/her favourite holiday place.

What … favourite holiday place?
Where …?
How … get there?
What … like best about it?

## 16.2 Exercise 2

Student B answers

**HAVE FUN ON OUR SCHOOL TRIP TO BRIGHTON**

Only £12.50 for students at this school!

Price includes lunch and return coach journey

Free time for shopping or visiting the beach

Saturday 7 April (book by Wednesday 4 April)

## 20.2 Exercise 5

Student B questions

Ask Student A about his/her luckiest moment.

What … was your luckiest moment?
When … happen?
Why … happen?
How … feel?
What … do afterwards?

# Grammar folder

## Unit 1

### Yes/No questions in the present

- With **have got**, the *have* comes first and *got* comes after the subject.
  ***Have** you **got** any money with you?*

- With **be**, the verb comes first.
  ***Is** Giulio one of your friends?*

- With **can**, the verb comes first.
  ***Can** I borrow your music magazine?*

- With **other verbs**, we start the question with *Do* or *Does* and the main verb comes after the subject.
  ***Do** you **want** a cup of coffee?*
  ***Does** Sandro **help** you with your homework?*

**1A** Change the word order to make *Yes/No* questions.

1 got / my CD / you / have
   *Have you got my CD?*
2 tomorrow / your sister / come / can
3 Carmen and Maria / are / Brazil / from
4 like / dogs / you / do
5 it / time / to go / is
6 Arturo / catch / does / the same bus

### Wh- questions in the present

- With **be**, **have got** and **can**, the verb comes after the question word.
  *What's the time?*
  *Who **have** you **got** in your maths class?*
  *How **can** I get to your house?*

- With **other verbs**, *do* or *does* comes after the question word. The subject comes next and the main verb comes after the subject.
  *Why **do you want** my phone number?*
  *When **does Jana get** home?*

**1B** Make *Wh-* questions.

1 When / meet me / can
   *When can you meet me?*
2 How / get to school / do
3 Where / your house / is
4 What / in your bag / have got
5 Why / angry / are
6 Who / know / Ingrid / does

### Suggestions

- We use **Why don't/doesn't ...** to make suggestions.
  ***Why don't** we meet at school?*
  ***Why doesn't** Ruth come with us?*

- We also use **How about ...** to make suggestions. (Use the *-ing* verb after.)
  ***How about** seeing a film tonight?*

# Unit 2

*Some/any*

- We use **some** with uncountable nouns in affirmative sentences.
  *I've got **some** toothpaste.*

- We use **some** with countable nouns in affirmative sentences.
  *That shop has got **some** new computer games for sale.*

- We use **some** for a request.
  *Can I look at **some** trainers?*

- We always use **any** in negative sentences.
  *We don't sell **any** newspapers.*

- We usually use **any** in questions.
  *Have you got **any** city maps?*

2 Complete the sentences with *some* or *any*.

1 I'd like ...*some*... tennis balls, please.
2 There aren't ............... DVDs to borrow.
3 Have you got ............... shops near your flat?
4 Can I buy ............... apples?
5 I want ............... lemon shampoo.
6 Is there ............... juice left?
7 We've got ............... small sizes in the sale.
8 Do you get ............... emails advertising things?

# Unit 3

## Present simple

We use the present simple to talk about:

- what we do every day
  *I **have breakfast** at 7.30 am.*

- facts
  *Newsagents **sell** magazines.*
  *Cats **eat** fish.*

| affirmative |
| --- |
| I/You/We/They **drink** coffee. |
| He/She/It **drinks** water. |

| question |
| --- |
| What **do** I/you/we/they **eat**? |
| What **does** he/she/it **drink**? |

| negative |
| --- |
| I/You/We/They **don't eat (do not eat)** potatoes. |
| He/She/It **doesn't drink (does not drink)** water. |

3 Complete the sentences using the verb in brackets.

1 I ...*prefer*... (prefer) coffee to tea.
2 ............... Pete really ............... (hate) carrots?
3 Both Katie and Jack ............... (love) chocolate.
4 My brother ............... (not eat) vegetables.
5 Rachel ............... (go) to restaurants three times a week.
6 ............... you usually ............... (go) to a party on New Year's Eve?
7 Supermarkets ............... (not sell) computers.

# Unit 4

## Past simple

We use the past simple to talk about:

- things that happened in the past
  *He **travelled** around the world.*

- past states
  *It **was** a long journey.*
  *He **liked** China.*

### The verb *be*

| affirmative |
| --- |
| You/We/They **were** right. |
| I/He/She/It **was** right. |

| question |
| --- |
| **Was** I/he/she/it right? |
| **Were** you/we/they right? |
| Yes, I/he/she/it **was**. |
| Yes, you/we/they **were**. |
| No, I/he/she/it **wasn't (was not)**. |
| No, you/we/they **weren't (were not)**. |

| negative |
| --- |
| I/He/She/It **wasn't (was not)** right. |
| You/We/They **weren't (were not)** right. |

### Regular verbs, e.g. *arrive*

| affirmative |
| --- |
| I/You/He/She/It/We/They **arrived** home. |

| question |
| --- |
| **Did** I/you/he/she/it/we/they **arrive** home? |
| Yes, I/you/he/she/it/we/they **did**. |
| No, I/you/he/she/it/we/they **didn't (did not)**. |

| negative |
| --- |
| I/you/he/she/it/we/they **didn't arrive (did not arrive)** home. |

### Irregular verbs, e.g. *meet*

Many verbs are irregular in the past tense, for example *meet – met*. See the list on page 151.

| affirmative |
| --- |
| I/You/He/She/It/We/They **met** the king. |

| question |
| --- |
| **Did** I/you/he/she/it/we/they **meet** the king? |
| Yes, I/you/he/she/it/we/they **did**. |
| No, I/you/he/she/it/we/they **didn't (did not)**. |

| negative |
| --- |
| I/You/He/She/It/We/They **didn't meet** the king. |

4   Complete the sentences using the verb in brackets in the past simple.

1 How long *did you stay* (you stay) in London?
2 ................................ (you enjoy) the boat trip?
3 The coach ................................ (not arrive) back at school on time.
4 My mother ................................ (make) me some sandwiches to take on the trip.
5 We ................................ (travel) to Rome by plane.
6 What ................................ (Lyn see) when she ................................ (go) to New York?
7 He ................................ (not speak) Spanish at all on his holiday.
8 Where ................................ (she buy) that souvenir?

# Unit 5

## Conjunctions

*and  but  or  because*

We use conjunctions to join two clauses or sentences to make one longer sentence.

Sentence A    *Polar bears weigh from 350 to 650 kg.*  **AND**

Sentence B    *Polar bears are two and a half metres to three metres long.*

*Polar bears weigh from 350 to 650 kg and are two and a half to three metres long.*

- We use **and** when we want to *add* one fact or idea to another.
  *I saw a polar bear **and** there were two cubs with her.*

- We use **but** when there is a *contrast* between the two facts or ideas.
  *I saw a polar bear **but** he was asleep.*

- We use **or** when there is a *choice* or an alternative fact or idea.
  *You can go to the zoo **or** stay at home.*

- We use **because** to say *why* things happen.
  *I gave the penguin some fish **because** it was hungry.*
  ***Because** the penguin was hungry, I gave it some fish.*

5  **Complete these sentences using *and, but, or* or *because*.**

1  Dogs like going for long walks ......*and*...... also playing with sticks.
2  My cat is getting old, ................. she still chases birds.
3  I took my dog to the vet ................. she was ill.
4  The elephants I saw in India worked in the early morning ................. slept in the afternoon.
5  ................. I live in a flat, I can't have a pet.
6  Would you like a cat as a pet ................. would you prefer a dog?

# Unit 6

## Comparative and superlative adjectives

| adjective | comparative | superlative |
|---|---|---|
| **short words** | | |
| tall | taller | the tallest |
| big | bigger | the biggest |
| easy | easier | the easiest |
| **long words** | | |
| expensive | more/less expensive | the most/least expensive |
| **exceptions** | | |
| good | better | the best |
| bad | worse | the worst |

*Theme parks in the USA are **bigger than** the ones in the UK.*
*My ticket was **more expensive** this year **than** last.*
*I think Disneyland is **the best** theme park.*

6  **Complete these sentences with either the comparative or the superlative form of the adjective in brackets.**

1  The park was ......*busier*...... (busy) on Saturday than on Sunday.
2  It's ................. (expensive) for children to get into the park than it is for adults.
3  The ride I went on was ................. (tall) in the park.
4  My uncle is ................. (rich) than I am so he paid for my trip to Disneyland Paris.
5  It was ................. (sunny) on Tuesday than it was on Monday.
6  The ................. (popular) ride was Inferno.
7  The ride was ................. (fast) in the park.
8  The theme park was ................. (expensive) than the one I usually go to.
9  Some theme parks are ................. (good) than others.
10  The hotel I stayed in was ................. (bad) in the area.

# Unit 7

## Simple and continuous tenses

- We use the **present continuous** to talk about **something temporary**, that is true now but not in general. Compare these sentences:
  *I'm wearing a skirt today because I've got an interview.*
  *I usually wear jeans.*

- We can use the **past continuous** to talk about a **temporary situation in the past**. Compare this with the **past simple**, which we use for a **completed action**:
  *Most people were wearing Roma shirts at last week's match.*
  *Roma won last week's match 2–0.*

- We also use the **past continuous** to talk about **something which continued before or after** another action.
  *I was shopping for shoes when my mobile phone rang.*

7 Put the verbs in brackets in the correct past tense.

1 Helena ....*was looking at*.... (look at) jackets when I ....*met*.... (meet) her.
2 I ............................ (try on) my new dress when the zip ............................ (break) .
3 John ............................ (queue) to pay when he ............................ (remember) his wallet was at home.
4 Martina ............................ (choose) her meal when the fire alarm ............................ (go off).
5 Maria ............................ (study) in the garden when it ............................ (begin) to rain.
6 When my friend ............................ (phone), I ............................ (have) a shower, so she ............................ (leave) me a message.

# Unit 8

## Modal verbs 1

*must*

- In the present, we use *must* to talk about obligation.
  *You must finish your homework before you go out.*

- In the past, we cannot use *must*. Instead, we use *had to*.
  *I had to queue for twenty minutes at the cinema.*

*may*

- We use *may* to talk about possibility.
  *I may come with you tonight.*

*can* and *could*

- In the present, we use *can* to talk about ability.
  *I can ride a bike.* (= I know how to ride a bike.)
  *I can't drive.* (= I don't know how to drive.)

- In the past tense, we use *could* and *couldn't*.
  *Sam could play the guitar before he was 12.*
  *He couldn't read music when he was at school.*

8 Complete the sentences using each modal verb once only.

| can | can't | ~~couldn't~~ | had to | may | must |
|-----|-------|--------------|--------|-----|------|

1 Giacomo didn't know how to find the cinema.
  Giacomo ....*couldn't*.... find the cinema.
2 Perhaps I'll come to the theatre tonight.
  I ............................ come to the theatre tonight.
3 Please wear a white shirt and black trousers at tonight's concert.
  You ............................ wear a white shirt and black trousers at tonight's concert.
4 Sorry, but I'm busy next Friday.
  I ............................ go out with you next Friday.
5 The front door of the club was locked.
  We ............................ use the back door of the club.
6 I know how to play the drums.
  I ............................ play the drums.

# Unit 9

## The future with *going to*

- We use *to be going to* to talk about plans and arrangements which are definite.

| affirmative | | |
|---|---|---|
| I | am | |
| He/She/It | is | going to swim every day. |
| You/We/They | are | |

| question | | |
|---|---|---|
| Am | I | |
| Is | he/she/it | going to walk up the hill? |
| Are | you/we/they | |

| negative | | |
|---|---|---|
| I | 'm not | |
| He/she/it | isn't | going to sleep in a tent. |
| We/you/they | aren't | |

| question | |
|---|---|
| Aren't I/we/you/they | |
| Isn't he/she | going to book a room? |
| Note: Am I not becomes Aren't I. | |

*I'm going to stay in a traditional house when I'm in Japan.*
*He isn't going to spend a lot of money on an expensive hotel.*
*Sam's going to take one small suitcase with him when he goes on holiday next week.*

## The future with *will*

- We use *will* to give information about the future or guess what will happen in the future.

| affirmative and negative |
|---|
| I/you/he/she/it/we/they **will** / **will not** (**won't**) travel. |

| question and negative |
|---|
| **Will/won't** I/you/he/she/it/we/they travel? |

*One day people **will** live on Mars.*

- We often use *will* with sentences beginning *I think …* and with adverbs like *certainly* (100%), *definitely* (100%), *probably* (about 70%) and *possibly* (about 40%).
*I think I will/I'll get a holiday job next year.*
*I will/I'll probably work in a hotel.*
*I don't think I'll earn a lot of money.*
*I probably won't spend a lot of money.*

9 Use *be going to* or *will* in these sentences.

1 I ___*am going to*___ go to Sicily for my holidays next month – I already have my ticket.
2 Congratulations! I hear you and Theresa ........................ get married.
3 What do you think you ........................ study when you go to university?
4 I ........................ have a party on Saturday – do you want to come?
5 The Lunar Hotel ........................ probably be the first hotel in space.
6 Claire thinks she ........................ definitely go abroad next year.
7 Maria ........................ take her driving test next week and she's very nervous.
8 I don't think people ........................ enjoy living on the moon very much.
9 I think air travel ........................ become much cheaper in the future.
10 Maria ........................ buy a new camera to take with her on holiday.

# Unit 10

## The passive

| | am/is/are (not) | + past participle painted |
|---|---|---|
| present simple passive | | |
| past simple passive | was/were (not) | seen built made |

The sentence *I painted my bedroom black* is active. The sentence *My bedroom was painted black* is passive.

- We often use *by* with the passive to tell us who did the action.
  *My bedroom was painted by my father.*
- The past participle of regular verbs ends in *-ed*, like the past tense.
- See page 151 for a list of past participles of irregular verbs.

10 Make sentences in the passive using A, B and C.

EXAMPLE: *The song 'Imagine' was sung by John Lennon.*

| | A | B | C |
|---|---|---|---|
| 1 | The song 'Imagine' | stop | by J. K. Rowling. |
| 2 | Spanish | give | in sweet shops. |
| 3 | The computer | win | to swim by my father. |
| 4 | The *Harry Potter* books | sing | by Brazil in 2002. |
| 5 | Presents | sell | in Peru. |
| 6 | Spaghetti | teach | by John Lennon. |
| 7 | I | invent | on birthdays. |
| 8 | Chocolate | eat | by Charles Babbage. |
| 9 | The World Cup | speak | all over the world. |
| 10 | The car | write | by the police. |

# Unit 11

## Verbs in the *-ing* form

- The *-ing* form is added to the infinitive of the verb:
  play + -ing = playing    *I enjoy **playing** tennis.*
- Different groups of verbs are followed by a verb in the *-ing* form:
  - verbs of liking and disliking:
    *enjoy, like*, love*, hate, don't mind, feel like*
      *I don't mind **getting** to the match early.*
      *I feel like **taking** it easy for an hour.*
  - verbs of doing:
    *keep, spend time*
      *He kept **asking** questions.*
      *We spent the day **fishing**.*
  - verbs of starting and stopping:
    *begin*, start*, finish, stop*
      *They stopped **talking** immediately.*
- * these verbs can also take an infinitive with no change of meaning:
  *I like **to listen** to the football scores at 5 o'clock.*
  *The team starts **to train** harder two days before a match.*

11 Complete the sentences with the *-ing* form of the verb in brackets.

1 I don't mind ....*coming*.... (come) with you to basketball training.
2 I feel like ...................... (swim) in the river – shall we go now?
3 Harry likes ...................... (choose) the team himself.
4 Do you enjoy ...................... (use) the gym equipment?
5 Kate can't stand ...................... (sit) and ...................... (watch) – she prefers to play in every match.
6 I hope Jenny doesn't mind ...................... (get) wet – it's going to rain!
7 How about ...................... (run) in the park before dinner?
8 Most racing drivers hate ...................... (drive) in heavy rain.

# Unit 12

## Pronouns

- There are different forms of personal pronouns:

| subject pronouns | object pronouns | reflexive pronouns |
|---|---|---|
| I | me | myself |
| you | you | yourself |
| he, she, it | him, her, it | himself, herself, itself |
| we | us | ourselves |
| you | you | yourselves |
| they | them | themselves |

- These are also pronouns:

| things | people |
|---|---|
| something | somebody / someone |
| anything | anybody / anyone |
| everything | everybody / everyone |
| nothing | nobody / no one |

- Remember that you must use a positive verb with *nothing*, *nobody* and *no one*.
  **I've got nothing** to read on the train.
  (= **I haven't got anything** to read on the train.)

- The relative pronouns **who** (people) and **which** (things) give more information in a sentence.
  *Hannah,* **who** *is Robin's sister, is in hospital.*
  *There's going to be a special birthday lunch,* **which** *is booked for 1.15.*

12 Complete the second sentences using suitable pronouns from those above.

1 Jenny came to the party alone.
  She didn't come with ........*anyone*........ .
2 David knows the whole truth.
  I've told him ............................ .
3 There's a phone message for you.
  ............................ from work called you.
4 I'm sure I can help.
  There's ............................ I can do.
5 All my family came to the party.
  ............................ was there.
6 The bus was empty.
  There was ............................ on it.

# Unit 13

## Adverbs of degree: *enough* and *too*
**adjective + *enough***
*I don't want to go swimming. It isn't* **hot enough.**
***too* + adjective**
*Can you close the window? It's* **too cold** *in here.*

- We can also use *to* + infinitive after *too* and *enough* with adjectives or adverbs.
  *It's hot enough* **to fry** *an egg.*
  *It's too far* **to walk.**

13 Complete the sentences with *too* or *enough* and the adjective in brackets.

1 It's ....*too dangerous*.... (dangerous) to go out side if there's a tornado.
2 It's ............................ (dry) here to grow tomatoes.
3 The ice isn't ............................ (thick) to go skating.
4 The sun isn't ............................ (hot) to heat the water in the pool.
5 The fog is ............................ (thick) to see the trees.
6 The wind was ............................ (strong) to go sailing.

# Unit 14

## Position of adjectives

- Sometimes we use two or more adjectives together. We put the 'opinion' adjective(s) first, and the 'fact' adjective(s) after.
  *The story is about a nice young man.*

- If there is more than one fact adjective, there are rules about the order they go in.

| 1 What's it like? *opinion* | 2 How big? *size* | 3 How old? *age* | 4 What colour? | 5 Where's it from? *nationality* | 6 What kind? | NOUN |
|---|---|---|---|---|---|---|
| great | | new | | | electric | guitar |
| | tall | | | American | | boy |
| | large | | white | | | house |

14 Put the adjectives in brackets in the correct place.

1 a old building  (lovely)
   *a lovely old building*
2 a wooden reading desk (large)
3 a popular American magazine (music)
4 an interesting story (adventure)
5 a friendly detective (young)
6 my French comic book (favourite)

# Unit 15

## Present perfect

- The present perfect is formed with:
  *have ('ve) / has ('s) + past participle*
  I **have worked** as a waiter.
  I**'ve seen** an interesting job advert.
  The manager **has sent** me an application form.

- Be careful with the past participle forms of irregular verbs! See the table on page 151.

- We use the present perfect
  – for something that started in the past but is still true:
  I**'ve broken** my arm. (= it's still broken)

  – for something that happened recently (but we don't know when):
  Alan**'s left** for work.

- The words *for* and *since* show how long something has been true:
  I've worked here **for** four months.
  I've worked here **since** August.

- The word *just* shows that something happened only a short time ago:
  The bus has **just** gone.

15 Rewrite these sentences using the present perfect and *just*.

1 Tyler began working as a chef last week.
   *Tyler has just begun working as a chef.*
2 Joan took the customer's order five minutes ago.
3 Giorgio recently became a doctor.
4 Someone left a message for you a couple of minutes ago.
5 I saw your mother crossing the street a few seconds ago.
6 I spoke to the mechanic on the phone a few minutes ago.

# Unit 16

## Modal verbs 2

### should

- We can use **should** (and **shouldn't**) to give advice.
  *You **should** walk to school – it's good exercise.*
  *You **shouldn't** come by car – it's better to walk.*

### must

- We use **must** to talk about obligation.
  *You **must** buy a ticket before you get on the bus.*
- We use **mustn't** to talk about things that aren't allowed.
  *You **mustn't** get on the bus without a ticket.*

### need to

- We use **need to** to talk about something necessary.
  *You **need to** check the train times on Saturdays.*

### don't have to, needn't

- We use **don't have to** and **needn't** when something is not necessary (when there is no obligation).
  *You **don't have to** show your ticket to the driver.*
  *You **needn't** wait for me on the platform. I'll see you on the train.*

16 Find the pairs of sentences that have the same meaning.

1 You don't have to book a seat on the train. *6*
2 You mustn't have a cigarette on the train.
3 You should take something to read on the train.
4 You need to arrive early for the train.
5 Smoking is forbidden on the train.
6 You needn't reserve a place on the train. *1*
7 You shouldn't arrive just before the train leaves.
8 Why not bring a book for the train?

# Unit 17

## Infinitive of purpose

- We often use the infinitive (**to** + **verb**) to say *why* we do things.
  *Liz needed a new bed.*
  *She went to a large furniture store.*
  *Liz went to a large furniture store **to buy** a new bed.*

17 Make one sentence using a phrase from A and a phrase from B.

EXAMPLE: *I went to the bus stop to catch a bus to town.*

| A | B |
|---|---|
| 1 I went to the bus stop | to pass the exam. |
| 2 I turned on the radio | to buy a CD. |
| 3 I went to the museum | to take to the party. |
| 4 I borrowed some money | to see an exhibition. |
| 5 I worked hard | to listen to the news. |
| 6 I bought a cake | to catch a bus to town. |

# Unit 18

## First conditional

- The first conditional is formed with:
  *If* + present tense + *will* + infinitive
- We use this structure to express a possible condition.
  **If** he **goes** swimming every day, he**'ll get fit**.
  (comma after the 'if' clause)
  We can also say:
  **He'll get fit if** he **goes** swimming every day.
  (no comma)

**18 Complete these sentences.**

1 If you (sleep) ......*sleep*...... with the window open, you (sleep much better) ......*you'll sleep much better*...... .

2 If you (eat) .......................... an apple a day, you (not get) ............................................ ill.

3 If you (not eat) .......................... too many sweets, you (not get fat)
   ............................................................ .

4 You (lose) .......................... weight if you (stop eating snacks) ............................................ .

5 Your teeth (stay) .......................... healthy if you (visit the dentist regularly)
   ............................................................ .

6 You (have) .......................... bad dreams if you (eat cheese in the evening)
   ............................................................ .

# Unit 19

## Prepositions of place and time

### Place

- We use **at** to talk about a specific place:
  *We're meeting **at** the stadium.*
  *Who's that standing **at** the bus stop?*
- We also use **at** to talk about places where you study or work:
  *Jane's studying Greek **at** university.*
- We use **on** to talk about where something is:
  *My bag is **on** the table.*
  *There's another bottle **on** the shelf.*
- We can use **in** or **on** with street names (but not for addresses):
  *I live **on** Madison Avenue.*
  *I live **at** 495 Madison Avenue.*
- We use **in** to talk about where something is:
  *There's a present for you **in** this box.*
  *Carrie's **in** the garden if you want to speak to her.*
- We use **in** with cities and countries:
  *I studied French **in** Paris.*
  *Uppsala is **in** Sweden.*

**19A Complete the sentences with *at, in* or *on*.**

1 I left my coat ...*on*... the chair. Could you get it?
2 Where's Punta Arenas? – It's ............ Chile.
3 I'm meeting Sam ............ the college gates.
4 James is living ............ London.
5 How long will you be ............ work? – I won't be free until six.
6 There's a new jazz club ............ Hilton Road.

## Time

- We use **at** with exact times, periods of time, meals and festivals:
  *Come round **at** five o'clock.*
  *We'll be free **at** the weekend.*
  *Kelly sat with John **at** breakfast.*
  *I'm doing a French course **at** Easter.*

- We use **in** with centuries, years, months, seasons and parts of the day:
  *Cornish was spoken widely **in** the 18th century.*
  *The book first came out **in** 2003.*
  *I went to Milan **in** January.*
  *It gets very busy here **in** summer.*
  *Shall we meet **in** the morning?*

- We use **on** with days of the week, dates and special days:
  *I have Spanish classes **on** Tuesday and Thursday.*
  *The party will be **on** 27 June.*
  ***On** Bonfire Night, there are lots of fireworks.*

**19B** Complete the sentences with *at*, *in* or *on*.

1 Will I see you ...*in*... March?
2 My birthday's ............ September 30.
3 Dani's going to visit us ............ Christmas.
4 What do you like to do ............ the evening?
5 I can't go to the theatre ............ Saturday.
6 This house was built ............ 1872.
7 Your appointment is ............ 3.15.
8 You can't swim here ............ winter.

# Unit 20
## Review of tenses

**Present simple**
*I like David Beckham.*
*Most people wear jeans.*
→ **See Unit 3**

**Present continuous**
*I'm reading an adventure story.*
→ **See Unit 7**

**Past simple**
*Leonardo da Vinci designed a helicopter.*
→ **See Unit 4**

**Past continuous**
*We were having a picnic when it started to rain.*
→ **See Unit 7**

**Present perfect**
*I've just had a text message from my brother.*
→ **See Unit 15**

**Future with *will***
*We'll meet in London for your birthday.*
→ **See Unit 9**

**Future with *going to***
*I'm going to have a bath and go to bed.*
→ **See Unit 9**

**20** Complete the sentences in the correct tense, using a verb from the box.

| catch   drive   eat   go out   make   sing |
|---|

1 Before she was famous, Pink ...*sang*... in an all-girl band called *Choice*.
2 Madonna ...................... a new CD – it'll go on sale next month.
3 Do you think Robbie Williams ...................... with Lisa Scott-Lee?
4 When she was on her diet, Nicole Kidman only ...................... spinach and egg whites.
5 The police ...................... Justin Timberlake when he ...................... too fast. He had to pay a fine.

# Vocabulary folder

Here are lists of the most useful words to learn from each unit. Some words are in more than one list.

## Unit 1

**Things you do with friends**
borrow (a CD from someone)
forget/remember (a birthday)
get/send a text (message)
go on PlayStation
go shopping
lend (someone a DVD)
tell a lie

**Adjectives**
angry
boring
free
funny
ill
pleased
sad
special

## Unit 2

**Places to go shopping**
bookshop
chemist
department store
market
newsagent
supermarket

**Uncountable nouns**
aspirin
chocolate
leather
make-up
money
shampoo
shopping
toothpaste

**Countable nouns**
book
box (boxes)
camera
dish (dishes)
magazine
map
newspaper
potato (potatoes)
sweets
tomato (tomatoes)

## Unit 3

**Food and drink**
apple
banana
biscuits
bread
burger
cake
carrot
cheese
chicken
chocolate
coffee
fish
fruit
grape
ice cream
lemonade
meat
onion
orange
orange juice
pasta
pizza
potato
rice
salad
sandwich
soup
steak
tea
tomato
water

**Meals**
breakfast
lunch
dinner

**Verbs**
drink
eat

**Verb + noun**
have a drink
have (a) pizza
make a meal

## Unit 4

**Verbs**
arrive
go by ship
return
stay
travel
visit

## Unit 5

**Animals**
bear
bird
cat
cow
dog
dolphin
elephant
fish
horse
monkey
spider

**Verb + noun**
do homework
do nothing
do the shopping
make an appointment
make a cake
make a phone call
make some money
spend time
take a photograph
take an exam

## Unit 6

**Adjectives**
bad
beautiful
big
boring
cheap
closed
easy
expensive
fast
good
happy
new
old
open
popular

short
small
tall
thin

**Adverbs**
badly
early
fast
hard
high
late
long
near
soon
well

**Things you do in your free time**
go cycling
go dancing
go shopping
go skateboarding
listen to CDs
play chess
play computer games
play table tennis
read comics
see friends
watch TV

# Unit 7

**Clothes**
baseball cap
belt
blouse
boots
button
coat
dress
hat
jacket
jeans
pocket
shirt
shoes
shorts

skirt
socks
suit
sweater
T-shirt
trainers
trousers
zip

**Adjectives**
cheap
clean
cotton
dirty
expensive
fashionable
heavy
large
leather
light
long
new
old
short
small
unfashionable
wool

# Unit 8

**Cinema**
actor
film
movie
scene
special effects
story

**Music**
band
bass
concert
drums
guitar
lights
piano
singer
speakers

# Unit 9

**Kinds of holiday**
a beach/camping/
cycling/walking holiday

**Places**
campsite
holiday home
holiday centre
hotel

**Verbs**
go/travel by plane,
  by car, by boat

# Unit 10

**The home**
bathroom
bedroom
dining room
garage
hall
kitchen
living room

**Things in a room**
bed
bookshelf
CD player
chair
computer
curtains
desk
DVD player
floor
lamp
light
mirror
poster
sofa
wardrobe

**Materials**
cotton
glass
gold
leather

metal
paper
plastic
silver
wood
wool

**Adjectives**
double
hard
high
little
long
low
narrow
quiet
single
soft
wide

**Colours**
black
blue
brown
green
grey
orange
pink
purple
red
white
yellow

# Unit 11

**Sports**
baseball
basketball
football
golf
horse-riding
sailing
skiing
snowboarding
swimming
volleyball
windsurfing

**Football words**
club
cup
goal
kick (noun and verb)
match
net
referee
score (noun and verb)
striker
team

**Sports equipment**
ball
basket
board
boots
gloves
net
racket

# Unit 12

**Family**
aunt
brother
cousin
dad(dy)
daughter
father
grandchild
granddaughter
grandfather (granddad)
grandmother (grandma)
grandson
mother
mum(my)
sister
son
uncle

# Unit 13

**Weather**
cloud(y)
cold
dry
fog(gy)
ice/icy
rain(y)/raining
snow(y)
storm(y)
sun(ny)
thunderstorm
tornado
warm
wet
wind(y)

# Unit 14

**Kinds of reading material**
adventure story
book
comic
detective story
love story
picture book
science fiction book

**Subjects**
art
geography
history
languages
maths
music
science
sport

# Unit 15

**Jobs**
actor
artist
chef
cleaner
dentist
doctor
farmer
footballer
journalist
mechanic
nurse
photographer
receptionist
secretary
shop assistant
teacher
tennis player
tour guide
waiter

**People at work**
boss
colleague
manager
staff

# Unit 16

**Transport**
airport
bicycle (bike)
boat
bus
car
coach
helicopter
horse
plane
ship
taxi
train

**Verbs**
board
catch
drive
fly
get (on/off)
park
ride
sail
take off

# Unit 17

**Technology**
chat room
computer
gadget
internet
laptop
mobile phone
robot
text message
video

**Verbs**
be online
call
check email
email
set the video
switch on
text
turn on

**Verb + noun**
get a job
make a film
make a noise
make friends
see a film
see friends
watch a film
watch TV

# Unit 18

**Parts of the body**
arm
back
ear
eye
foot
hair
hand
head
leg
mouth
neck
nose

**Health**
ambulance
chemist
doctor
hospital
medicine
nurse
sick
temperature

**Verb + noun**
have a broken arm
a cold
a cut
a headache
a sore throat
stomach ache
toothache

**Other verb phrases**
get fit
go on a diet
go to sleep
sleep well
wake up

# Unit 19

**Communication**
email
envelope
fax
letter
mobile phone
note
postcard
stamp
telephone
text

**Languages**
Arabic
Chinese
Danish
Dutch
Flemish
French
Gaelic

German
Greek
Italian
Japanese
Norwegian
Polish
Portuguese
Russian
Spanish
Swedish
Turkish

# Unit 20

**Winning**
competition
luck
prize

**Adjectives**
angry
clever
famous
happy
kind
lucky
married
single
special

# Irregular verbs

| Infinitive | Past simple | Past participle |
|---|---|---|
| be | was/were | been |
| become | became | become |
| begin | began | begun |
| break | broke | broken |
| bring | brought | brought |
| build | built | built |
| burn | burnt/burned | burnt/burned |
| buy | bought | bought |
| catch | caught | caught |
| choose | chose | chosen |
| come | came | come |
| cost | cost | cost |
| cut | cut | cut |
| do | did | done |
| draw | drew | drawn |
| drink | drank | drunk |
| drive | drove | driven |
| eat | ate | eaten |
| fall | fell | fallen |
| feel | felt | felt |
| find | found | found |
| fly | flew | flown |
| forget | forgot | forgotten |
| get | got | got |
| give | gave | given |
| go | went | gone/been |
| grow | grew | grown |
| have | had | had |
| hear | heard | heard |
| hit | hit | hit |
| hurt | hurt | hurt |
| keep | kept | kept |
| know | knew | known |
| learn | learnt/learned | learnt/learned |
| leave | left | left |
| lend | lent | lent |
| lie | lay | lain |
| lose | lost | lost |
| make | made | made |
| mean | meant | meant |

| Infinitive | Past simple | Past participle |
|---|---|---|
| meet | met | met |
| pay | paid | paid |
| put | put | put |
| read | read | read |
| ride | rode | ridden |
| run | ran | run |
| say | said | said |
| see | saw | seen |
| sell | sold | sold |
| send | sent | sent |
| show | showed | shown |
| shut | shut | shut |
| sing | sang | sung |
| sit | sat | sat |
| sleep | slept | slept |
| speak | spoke | spoken |
| spell | spelt/spelled | spelt/spelled |
| spend | spent | spent |
| stand | stood | stood |
| steal | stole | stolen |
| swim | swam | swum |
| take | took | taken |
| teach | taught | taught |
| tell | told | told |
| think | thought | thought |
| throw | threw | thrown |
| understand | understood | understood |
| wake | woke | woken |
| wear | wore | worn |
| win | won | won |
| write | wrote | written |

# Acknowledgements

Once again the authors would like to give their warmest thanks to Alyson Maskell for her useful suggestions, encouragement and attention to detail. Thanks also go to Sue Ashcroft at Cambridge University Press for her constant diligence and support, and to Stephanie White at Kamae for her creative design solutions.

The authors and publishers would like to thank the teachers and students who trialled and commented on the material:

Argentina: Moira Mariana Valenti; Brazil: Margarida C. T. Busatto; Greece: Takis Loulakis; Italy: James Douglas, Teresa Ferrero Musso, Tim Julian, Charlotte Villiers; Japan: Alex Case; Mexico: Jan Isaksen; Spain: Gill Hamilton, Samantha Lewis, Chris Turner; UK: Sally Bowen, Paul Bress, Maureen Ellis, Nicola Gardner, Amanda Thomas.

The authors and publishers are grateful to the authors, publishers and others who have given permission for the use of copyright material identified in the text. It has not been possible to identify the sources of all the material used and in such cases the publishers would welcome information from copyright owners. Apologies are expressed for any omissions.

Text on p.69 adapted from a text by Ian Ridley from 'I live to score goals: Exclusive Interview: Michael Owen' written by Ian Ridley, published in The Observer, 29 September, 2002; text on p.123 IPC Media Ltd (IPC) for text from 'I'm gonna be Mrs Beckham', ©Mizz/IPC Syndication; text on p.128 adapted from Activity Box by Joan Greenwood © Cambridge University Press 1997.

The publishers are grateful to the following for permission to reproduce copyright photographs and material:

Key: l = left, c = centre, r = right, t = top, b = bottom, back = background, lo = lower, u = upper.

The Advertising Archive for p. 16 (r); ©2002 Amazon.com, Inc. All Rights Reserved for p. 16 (c); ©APEX/Simon Burt 123 (Jenna); Aquarius Collection/©Warner Brothers for pp. 50 (tr), 51, /©Twentieth Century Fox for p. 50 (bl), /©New Line Cinema for p. 50 (tr), /©Walt Disney for p. 54, /©MGM/EON for p. 106; Associated Press, AP/Itsuo Inouye for p. 39; Anthony Blake Photo Library/©Graham Salter for p. 126; ©Bubbles for pp. 92 (tl), 94; CORBIS/©Bob Rowan; Progressive Image for p. 23 (t), /©Jose Fuste Raga for pp. 28 (b), 64 (bc), /©Robert Holmes for p. 28 (uc), /©Ed Kash for p. 28 (loc), /©Phil Schermeister for p. 31 (t), /©Jason Hawkes for p. 38 (r), /©Scott T. Smith for p. 40, /©Michael Kevin Daly for p. 56 (tr), /©Paul Hardy for p. 65, /©Richard Cummins/Hearst Castle/CA Park Service for p. 66, /©Joseph Sohm: ChromoSohm Inc. for p. 67, /©Shaun Best/Reuters for p. 74, /©Richard Chung/Reuters for p. 80 (br), /©Robert Garvey for p. 114; ©Steve Davey for p. 22; EMPICS/©Curt Ylving/SCANPIX for p. 68 (bc), /©Simon Bellis for p. 69, /©Mike Egerton for p. 79; ©Warren Faidley/Stormchaser.com for p. 83; GettyImages/ImageBank/James Darell for p. 8 (tl), /Color Day Production for p. 80 (tr), /James Schnepf for p. 92 (br), /Sean Justice for p. 110 (man's back), /J.W. Buckey for p. 124; GettyImages/PhotoDisc Collection for p. 80 (tcl); GettyImages/Photographer's Choice/Shaun Egan for p. 64 (br), /Frank Cezus for p. 80 (l); GettyImages/Stone/Jerome Tisne for p. 9 (tr), /Stuart Hughs for p. 9 (cr), /Daniel J Cox for p. 34, /John Lawrence for p. 64 (tc), /Ralph Wetmore for p. 80 (bcl), /Dale Durfee for p. 88, /Paul Redman for p. 92 (tc); GettyImages/Taxi/Antonio Mo for p. 8 (cl), /Benelux Press for p. 8 (bl), /Ron Chapple for p. 9 (tl), /Sarah Hutchings for p. 9 (br), /Lisa Peardon for pp. 28 (t), 56 (c), /Gail Shumway for p. 37, /Burgess Blevins for p. 56 (br), /David Nardini for p. 56 (l), /Ken Ross for p. 65 (tl), /H.H for p. 64 (bl), /Adrian Lyon for p. 64 (tr), /David Greenwood for p. 80 (tcr), /Getty Images for pp. 80 (bcr), 110 (floor exercise), /Angela Scott for p. 102; ©Bernie Hayden for p. 76; PA Photos/©EPA European Press Agency for p. 112 (c, b); ©Popperfoto for pp. 68 (bl, tl), 122 (tr); ©Powerstock/Superstock for p. 8 (br), /©AGE Fotostock for pp. 95, 110 (face); Redferns/©Geoff Dann for p. 43, /©Christina Radish for p. 53; Rex Features p. 123 (Beckham), /Nick Cunard for p. 23 (b), /SIPA Press for pp. 35, 55, /Stuart Cook for p. 38 (l), /ADC for p. 44 (b),

/©Peter Brooker for p. 90 (bl), /©Nils Jorgensen for p. 122 (b); ©Sankei Shimbun for p. 105 (r); Science Photo Library/©Victor Habbick for p. 58, /©Adam Hart-Davis for p. 105 (l); ©Swim Shop for p. 16 (l); ©2000 Topham/Imageworks for p. 68 (tc); ©2001 Topfoto/PressNet for p. 68 (r), /©2002 Topfoto/PressNet for p. 122 (tl); ©2002 Topfoto/PA for pp. 38 (c), 92 (tr), /Keystone for p. 48, /UPPA.co.uk for p. 52; ©2003 Topfoto/POLFOTO/Thomas Borberg for p. 31 (b); ©2003 Topham/Imageworks for pp. 8 (cr), 9 (bl); The Random House Group Limited for the jacket cover of The Teenage Worrier's Guide to Life by Ros Asquith, © The Random House Group Limited 1997.

We have been unable to trace the copyright holder of the image on page 112 (t), and would appreciate any information to enable us to do so.

Commissioned photography organised by Val Mulcahy:
The photographs on pages 10, 20 (bottom), 44 (top), 60 and 86 are by Gareth Boden. The photographs on pages 14 and 20 (top), are by Paul Mulcahy.

Illustrations by:
James Brown pp 15 (tr), 20, 27, 32, 41, 47, 57, 68, 75, 95; Tim Davies pp. 8, 30, 62 (t), 81, 98 (t), 127; Francis Fung pp. 40, 46, 63, 116; Leanne Jackson pp. 29, 78, 88; Kamae Design (DTP) pp. 13, 15 (l), 21, 80, 98 (bl), 99, 101, 105, 118; Gillian Martin pp. 12, 13, 36, 82 (r), 90, 96, 111; Colin Mier pp. 17, 56, 128; Melanie Sharp pp. 23, 62 (b), 98 (br); Laszlo Veres p. 26; David Whittle pp. 52, 70, 82 (l), 84, 100, 104, 129, 135, 137, 140, 142, 144, 145, 146

Picture research by Hilary Fletcher.